# Kinder Kollege

Teacher's Guide

L. M. Logan
Patrice Juah
Ophelia S. Lewis

Village Tales Publishing
MINNEAPOLIS, MN

Copyright © 2020 by Liberia Literary Society
All rights reserved. No part of this publication may be reproduced, distributed or transmitted in any form or by any means, without prior written permission.

Village Tales Publishing
www.villagetalespublishing.com
www.oass.villagetalespublishing.com
www.villagetalespublishing.com/childrensbooks

Book Cover by OASS
ISBN 9781945408359
LCCN 2020905581

A Liberia Literary Society
Educational Project

Printed in the USA

# Contents

Notes on the Contributors ........................................................................... 6
Introduction ................................................................................................. 7
Kindergarten Benchmark ............................................................................. 8
## Teacher's Lesson Planners ................................................................. 13
## Language Arts - Guided Writing .......................................................... 36
   A Writer's Eye ......................................................................................... 41
   Types of Sentences ................................................................................ 42
   Rules for Capital Letters ........................................................................ 43
   Verbs Show Actions ............................................................................... 44
   Adjectives ............................................................................................... 45
   Sequencing ............................................................................................. 46
   How a Book is Made .............................................................................. 47
   The Writing Process .............................................................................. 48
   Opinion Writing ...................................................................................... 49
   Writing a Letter ...................................................................................... 51
   The Post Office ...................................................................................... 52
## Language Arts - Guided Spelling ......................................................... 53
   2-Letter Words ....................................................................................... 55
   3-Letter Words ....................................................................................... 55
   4-Letter Words ....................................................................................... 57
   5-Letter Words ....................................................................................... 58
   6-Letter Words ....................................................................................... 59
   7-Letter Words ....................................................................................... 59
   9-Letter Words ....................................................................................... 59
   8-Letter Words ....................................................................................... 59
   Compound Words ................................................................................... 60
   Synonym Words ..................................................................................... 61
   Antonym Words ..................................................................................... 62
## Language Arts - Guided Reading ........................................................ 63
   What is Reading? ................................................................................... 66
   Beginning Sounds .................................................................................. 67
   Short Vowel Sounds .............................................................................. 70
   Ending Sounds ....................................................................................... 72
   My Sounds Chart .................................................................................... 73
   Phonics Sounds ...................................................................................... 74
   My Blends Chart ..................................................................................... 76
   Beginning Blends .................................................................................... 77
   Ending Blends and Digraphs .................................................................. 77
   Rhyming .................................................................................................. 79
   Syllables .................................................................................................. 81
   Reading Fluency ..................................................................................... 82
   Focus on Fluency ................................................................................... 85

Fluency Rubric ...........................................................................................86
Reading Comprehension .........................................................................88
Read and Sequence ................................................................................98
Guided Reading Lesson Plan ................................................................103
**Primary Arithmetic** ...................................................................**104**
Math and Numbers ................................................................................107
Number Words .......................................................................................108
Addition Word List .................................................................................109
Subtraction Word List ...........................................................................109
Addition Strategies ...............................................................................110
Addition ..................................................................................................112
Subtraction Action ................................................................................118
Shapes ....................................................................................................120
Order ......................................................................................................124
Passage of Time Order ..........................................................................124
Place Preposition ...................................................................................125
Left and Right Position .........................................................................125
Occupying Space ...................................................................................126
Measuring Up! .......................................................................................127
Problem Solving ....................................................................................131
All About Time .......................................................................................132
Word Problems ......................................................................................134
Currency & Money .................................................................................135
Word Problems With LRDs (L$) .............................................................136
**Social Studies** ..........................................................................**137**
Our Nation ..............................................................................................138
Liberia's Counties, Capitals, and Flags ................................................139
Names of Our Presidents ......................................................................141
National Anthem ....................................................................................142
Who is a Patriot? ...................................................................................143
Voting and Election ...............................................................................144
Rules and Laws .....................................................................................147
Currency & Money .................................................................................148
Community Helpers & Volunteers ........................................................149
Volunteering ..........................................................................................150
**Science - Smart Start** .............................................................**151**
Science and Scientists ..........................................................................153
Scientific Methods ................................................................................154
Scientist Activities ................................................................................155
Weather Measurement Tools ................................................................156
Weather in Liberia .................................................................................158
Earth Science ........................................................................................159
Physical Science ...................................................................................162
Simple Machines ...................................................................................163
Force & Motion ......................................................................................164
Energy Science .....................................................................................165
Natural Energy Resources ....................................................................167

Life Science ........................................................................................................ 170
Man-made Vs. Natural ....................................................................................... 171
Gifts of the sun .................................................................................................. 172
Plants .................................................................................................................. 173
Plants in Our Lives ............................................................................................. 176
Animals ............................................................................................................... 177
Animal Babies Grow Up ..................................................................................... 178
Our Body ............................................................................................................. 179
Human Growth Stages ....................................................................................... 182
How to prevent malaria and stay well. .............................................................. 185
Bathroom Rules .................................................................................................. 187

# Technology .................................................................................**188**
Computer ............................................................................................................ 189
Desktop Computer ............................................................................................. 190
Laptop Computer ............................................................................................... 191
Research ............................................................................................................. 193
The Internet ....................................................................................................... 194
Online Digital Safety .......................................................................................... 195
Accessing Information ...................................................................................... 196
Technology ......................................................................................................... 199
Technology (Then and Now) ............................................................................. 201
Comparing Technology ...................................................................................... 202
Technology Spelling List ................................................................................... 203

# Primary Bible Lessons ................................................................**204**
The Bible ............................................................................................................. 205
The Creation ....................................................................................................... 206
The Golden Rule ................................................................................................. 207
All About Jesus .................................................................................................. 208
Psalm 23 .............................................................................................................. 212
How to Pray ........................................................................................................ 213
Fruit of the Spirit ............................................................................................... 214
Bible Stories ....................................................................................................... 215
52 Bible Verses to Memorize ............................................................................. 221

# Kinder Life Skills .......................................................................**224**
Five Character Traits ......................................................................................... 225
Being Independent ............................................................................................. 227
Friendship ........................................................................................................... 228
Honesty ............................................................................................................... 230
Sad, Mad, or Glad. .............................................................................................. 237
Safety .................................................................................................................. 238
Table Manners .................................................................................................... 242

# Motivating With Passion ............................................................**245**
What Makes a Teacher Great! ........................................................................... 245
How to be a Great Teacher ................................................................................ 247
Empowering Students ....................................................................................... 249

# Notes on the Contributors

**Manseen Logan** is a Liberian-American editor and writer. She published the first story in the "Adventures at Camp Pootie-Cho" children's book series. In the series, readers can learn about Liberia's endangered wildlife, the unique rainforest, and valuable life lessons. She enjoys participating in kids' book readings sponsored by Liberia Literary Society.

**Patrice Juah** is a communications professional, writer and editor. As founder of the Martha Juah Educational Foundation, she champions girls' education and leadership, through the foundation's academic initiative, Sexy Like A Book. An accomplished author, poet, and public speaker, her literary works cover a wide range of themes, to include personal life experiences, women's empowerment and humor. A firm believer in the transformative power of education, Juah contributes to the Liberia Literary Society and Village Tales Publishing, as board member and editor, respectively.

**Ophelia S. Lewis** is the CEO of the Liberia Literary Society organization, which provides resources to preserve Liberia's literary works, advance girls' education and youth development. Giving children a chance to learn is one of the most urgent priorities in Liberia. As a published author and humanitarian, Lewis takes on the dire, yet fulfilling task of giving children an opportunity to start a solid educational journey. Hopefully, the synergy of Liberia Literary Society and Village Tales Publishing will produce effective results for students. Quality education is key to any society's success; this ignites Lewis' passion for writing children's books.

# Introduction

What is Taught, When it is Taught, Who is Being Taught, and Who is Teaching, are critically important for kindergarteners. Teacher Jeanette offers Kindergarten students academic excellence from the perspective of the love for teaching and learning. With a strong emphasis on learning to read "phonetically," we believe children can gain the confidence to learn using the most updated educational materials while in a secure environment.

Kindergarten is the foundation of a child's education. The educational "house" a child builds in his/her life will be built on the foundation of kindergarten. It is during the first years of life that children form attitudes about themselves, others, learning, and the environment. Educating a child is most successful when teachers and schools work together in the best interest of the child. Valuing education and the opportunities it provides are important first steps. The goal of our workbooks is to meet students' needs not only intellectually, but also physically, socially, and emotionally.

Teacher Jeanette Kinder Kollege workbooks are packed with exercises that will make learning fun! These workbooks will provide a gentle introduction to structured learning that is both developmentally appropriate and academically foundational. They are proven activities to help prepare Liberian students for success; by teaching strong fundamentals to start their educational journey. Students will LOVE learning.

# Kindergarten Benchmark

1st Term
- Listens to a story
- Recognizes letters covered
- Draws recognizable pictures
- Recognizes likenesses/differences between objects, attributes
- Writes First Name
- Scribbles
- Recognizes front and back of a book, knows where to start on the page, knows to read from top to bottom (Book awareness)

2nd Term
- Uses random letters in writing
- Recognizes 16 upper/16 lowercase letters
- Writes 16 upper/16 lowercase letters
- Knows days of the week
- Uses directional/positional words
- Copies print
- Identifies rhyming words
- Knows most beginning sounds covered
- Counts to 30
- Recognizes story sequencing
- Knows character of the story
- Begins to retell a story
- Learns to point to words while reading

3rd Term
- Copies environmental print
- Describes likenesses/differences of shapes
- Writes using letter sounds consistently
- Recognizes ordinals to 10
- Compares objects and arranges in order
- Names shapes
- Recognizes and writes most letters
- Recognizes some sight words

- Tells a simple story that they know/created
- Begins to read or attempts to read a simple predictable or decodable text
- Knows the beginning, middle, and end of a story
- Recognizes ending sounds
- Knows months of the year

4th Term
- Recognizes 26 upper/26 lowercase letters
- Recognizes ending sounds
- Begins to recognize middle sounds
- Points to words while reading
- Writes words using letter sounds
- Writes Last Name
- Demonstrates a sense of the story by conveying its meaning

# WELCOME
## to kindergarten!!
**I'm so LUCKY to have you here!**

My name is Mr/Mrs/Ms _____.
I'm looking forward to being together with you this year. It's going to be a year full of fun, learning, and lots of adventures and I can't wait to see what the year has in store for us. I look forward to getting to know each of you and I thought you might like to know a little bit about me.

[say something about yourself]

I am so excited to teach you. I love teaching because students are at that wonderful stage of development, where they love to learn so much and I can be a part of their experience.

Please let me know if you have any questions or concerns. It is so important to keep communication open between us. Don't be afraid to come to talk to me about anything if you need to. I look forward to a great school year together.

**Here are a few of my favorites:**

| | |
|---|---|
| Favorite color | Favorite song |
| Favorite season | Favorite book |
| Favorite food | Favorite animal |
| Favorite drink | Favorite sport |
| Favorite hobby | Favorite movie |

# Kindergarten Rules

Follow Instructions
Use Quiet Voices
Keep Hands and Feet to Self
Respect Self, Others, and Property

**To do these in Kindergarten encourage students to...**

Smile a lot.
Always listen and look at the teacher when he/she talks.
Sit in their seat.
Be kind to others.
Raise their hand and wait to be called before talking.
Always walk in the classroom and the hall.
Stand in line correctly.
Follow all school rules.
Have a good time and learn.

# Consequences

**If student Does Not follow the rules:**
- 1st Time: student must get a verbal warning.
- 2nd Time: student must practice the appropriate behavior
- 3rd Time: use timeout isolation

**When studen follows the rules**
- Give the student verbal praises
- Students can receive rewards at the end of the week (movie, free time, candy, etc.)

## How to care for your book.

1. Read with clean hands.
2. Turn pages carefully.
3. Keep your book in your bookbag when you're not reading it.
4. Keep your book close to you when reading, so that you don't drop it.
5. Use a bookmark to save your page in a book.
6. Keep your book away from food and drinks.
7. Only draw, write, and color where instructed to.
8. Keep your book away from younger siblings and pets.

The first thing I do is always the same,
I pick up my pencil and write my name.

## Primary Handwriting Guidelines

  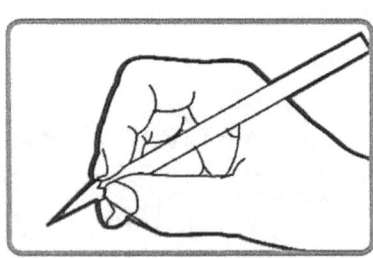

Sit down and place book flat in front of you.

Use your helper hand to hold the paper down while writing.

Correctly hold your pencil; only move the fingers when writing.

# TEACHER'S LESSON PLANNERS

**Seating Chart**

## Student Information

| First Name: | | | | | | |
|---|---|---|---|---|---|---|
| Last Name: | | | | | | |
| Birthday | | | | | | |
| | | | | | | |
| First Name: | | | | | | |
| Last Name: | | | | | | |
| Birthday | | | | | | |
| | | | | | | |
| First Name: | | | | | | |
| Last Name: | | | | | | |
| Birthday | | | | | | |
| | | | | | | |
| First Name: | | | | | | |
| Last Name: | | | | | | |
| Birthday | | | | | | |
| | | | | | | |
| First Name: | | | | | | |
| Last Name: | | | | | | |
| Birthday | | | | | | |
| | | | | | | |
| First Name: | | | | | | |
| Last Name: | | | | | | |
| Birthday | | | | | | |
| | | | | | | |
| First Name: | | | | | | |
| Last Name: | | | | | | |
| Birthday | | | | | | |
| | | | | | | |
| First Name: | | | | | | |
| Last Name: | | | | | | |
| Birthday | | | | | | |

©Teacher Jeanette Kinder Kollege

## Student Information

| First Name: | | | | | | |
|---|---|---|---|---|---|---|
| Last Name: | | | | | | |
| Birthday | | | | | | |
| | | | | | | |
| First Name: | | | | | | |
| Last Name: | | | | | | |
| Birthday | | | | | | |
| | | | | | | |
| First Name: | | | | | | |
| Last Name: | | | | | | |
| Birthday | | | | | | |
| | | | | | | |
| First Name: | | | | | | |
| Last Name: | | | | | | |
| Birthday | | | | | | |
| | | | | | | |
| First Name: | | | | | | |
| Last Name: | | | | | | |
| Birthday | | | | | | |
| | | | | | | |
| First Name: | | | | | | |
| Last Name: | | | | | | |
| Birthday | | | | | | |
| | | | | | | |
| First Name: | | | | | | |
| Last Name: | | | | | | |
| Birthday | | | | | | |
| | | | | | | |
| First Name: | | | | | | |
| Last Name: | | | | | | |
| Birthday | | | | | | |

©Teacher Jeanette Kinder Kollege

## Student Information

| First Name: | | | | | | |
|---|---|---|---|---|---|---|
| Last Name: | | | | | | |
| Birthday | | | | | | |
| | | | | | | |
| First Name: | | | | | | |
| Last Name: | | | | | | |
| Birthday | | | | | | |
| | | | | | | |
| First Name: | | | | | | |
| Last Name: | | | | | | |
| Birthday | | | | | | |
| | | | | | | |
| First Name: | | | | | | |
| Last Name: | | | | | | |
| Birthday | | | | | | |
| | | | | | | |
| First Name: | | | | | | |
| Last Name: | | | | | | |
| Birthday | | | | | | |
| | | | | | | |
| First Name: | | | | | | |
| Last Name: | | | | | | |
| Birthday | | | | | | |
| | | | | | | |
| First Name: | | | | | | |
| Last Name: | | | | | | |
| Birthday | | | | | | |
| | | | | | | |
| First Name: | | | | | | |
| Last Name: | | | | | | |
| Birthday | | | | | | |

©Teacher Jeanette Kinder Kollege

## Student Information

| | | | | | | |
|---|---|---|---|---|---|---|
| First Name: | | | | | | |
| Last Name: | | | | | | |
| Birthday | | | | | | |
| | | | | | | |
| First Name: | | | | | | |
| Last Name: | | | | | | |
| Birthday | | | | | | |
| | | | | | | |
| First Name: | | | | | | |
| Last Name: | | | | | | |
| Birthday | | | | | | |
| | | | | | | |
| First Name: | | | | | | |
| Last Name: | | | | | | |
| Birthday | | | | | | |
| | | | | | | |
| First Name: | | | | | | |
| Last Name: | | | | | | |
| Birthday | | | | | | |
| | | | | | | |
| First Name: | | | | | | |
| Last Name: | | | | | | |
| Birthday | | | | | | |
| | | | | | | |
| First Name: | | | | | | |
| Last Name: | | | | | | |
| Birthday | | | | | | |
| | | | | | | |
| First Name: | | | | | | |
| Last Name: | | | | | | |
| Birthday | | | | | | |

©Teacher Jeanette Kinder Kollege

# Primary Lesson Plan Guide

| Subject | 1st | 2nd | 3rd | 4th |
|---|---|---|---|---|
| Characher Education, Five character traits, Cognitive Development, Good behavior, Good Manners, Classroom Rules Social-emotional Maturity | | | | |
| Electives: Bible Stories, Art, Music, Coloring & Finger painting, Dancing, | | | | |
| Social Studies: Map and Globe, cardinal directions, Continents and Oceans, Latitude and Longitude, Compare similarities and differences, Where We Live, Good Citizenship, Community Helpers, Currency and Money, Making smart decisions, Counties, Capitals, and Flags, Liberian Flag, National Anthem Song, Names of Presidents, Liberian Symbols, Voting and Election | | | | |
| Language Arts - Writing: Begin with the Alphabets, pictures to spell words, What writers write, Building Sentences, Punctuation, Rules for Capital Letters, How a story is written, Parts of a Story, Narrative, Persuasive Writing - Opinions, Making a List, Label-put a word or words on something to identify, Written communication, write a letter, What is at the post office, Adjectives, Sequencing, Media center, Media Purpose, Digital Media, The Library, Writing to influence people, Grammar & Usage, Response to Literature, retell a story, Reference Skills | | | | |

©Teacher Jeanette Kinder Kollege

# Primary Lesson Plan Guide

| Subject | 1st | 2nd | 3rd | 4th |
|---|---|---|---|---|
| | | | | |
| Language Arts - Spelling Writing and Spelling begins with the Alphabets, UPPER CASE and lower case, Spell and write first and last name, Building words using Pyramids, Alphabetical Order, Rhyming, Word Lists, Number Words, Color Words, Patriotic Words, Weather Words, Clothing Words, Months of the Year, Days of the Week, school supply list, Word Smart Puzzles, Christmas Words, Social Relations Words, Fruits & Vegetables Words, Things at the Beach Words, Body Parts Words, Opposite Words | | | | |
| | | | | |
| Language Arts - Reading: Listening, Speaking, and Viewing, Respond to Questions, Follow two-part Directions, Participate in vocal speaking and creative drama, Recite short poems, rhymes, songs, and stories, Use oral language to relate experiences, Describe people, places, things, locations, and actions, Use complete sentences when speaking, Use subject-verb agreement and tense correctly, Reading Strategies and Comprehension, Make predictions from pictures and titles, S-O "SO" reading song, Relate written language to spoken language, Concepts About Print, Use of a pictionary or dictionary to identify words, match all consonant and short-vowel, Read first 50 high-frequency sight words and common words. | | | | |
| | | | | |

©Teacher Jeanette Kinder Kollege

# Primary Lesson Plan Guide

| Subject | 1st | 2nd | 3rd | 4th |
|---|---|---|---|---|
| | | | | |
| Technology, Technology at Home and School, Technology in Solving Problems, Technology word list, Technology Then and Now, Technology in Transportation, Travels by land, air, and water, Travel far and fast, Computers, What is a computer, Desktop and Laptop, Parts of a computer, Types of devices, Online Digital Safety, Staying safe online, protecting Private Information. | | | | |
| | | | | |
| Science: Characteristics of Science, Science and Scientists, The importance of curiosity, honesty, openness, and skepticism in science, Understand how the world works, Scientific processes and inquiry methods, Analyzing data and following scientific investigations, Tools and instruments for observing, measuring, and manipulating objects in scientific activities, The concepts of system, Communicate scientific ideas, Weather, Earth Science, Analyze time patterns and objects (sun, moon, stars) in the day and night sky, Physical attributes of rocks and soils, Landforms, Physical Science, States of Matter, Speed and direction, Push and pull, The effect of gravity on objects, Life Science, Plants and Animals, Distinguish living things from non-living things, Our body, Our five senses, Healthy Habits, Physical Education | | | | |
| | | | | |

©Teacher Jeanette Kinder Kollege

# Primary Lesson Plan Guide

| Subject | 1st | 2nd | 3rd | 4th |
|---|---|---|---|---|
|  |  |  |  |  |
| **Math:** Numbers and Operations, counting objects 1 through 30, Recognize and write numerals through 20, Sequence and identify ordinal numbers 1st through 10th, Estimate quantities using five and 10, Share objects equally between two or three people or sets, Identify LD/LRD by name and value: 5, 10, 20, 50,100 LD/LRD, Count out LD/LRD to buy items that together cost less than 50 LD/LRD, Make fair trades involving combinations of 5, 10, 20 LD/LRD, Geometry, Recognize, name, and sort geometric figures, Recognize and name spheres and cubes, Identify spatial relationships, such as when an object is beside, above, below, in front of, behind, inside, or outside another object, (Measurement) Compare and order objects on the basis of length(longer/shorter), capacity (more/less), height (taller/shorter), and weight (heavier/lighter), Name days of the week, months of the year, and the two seasons, Use the words yesterday, today, and tomorrow to describe passage of time order daily events, Tell the time when daily events occur, such as morning, afternoon, and night, (Algebra) Explore the concept of equivalence relating to addition and subtraction, Identifying attributes such as longer/shorter, more/less, taller/shorter, and heavier/lighter, and make generalizations, Collect and organize data, and record results using objects, pictures, and picture graphs |  |  |  |  |

©Teacher Jeanette Kinder Kollege

# Goals For School Year _____

| Character Education | Character Traits | Good Manners A -Z |
|---|---|---|
|  |  |  |
|  |  |  |
|  |  |  |
|  |  |  |
|  |  |  |
|  |  |  |
|  |  |  |
|  |  |  |
| The Alphabets | Spelling | Spelling |
|  | Word Building | Word Lists |
|  |  |  |
|  |  |  |
|  |  |  |
|  |  |  |
|  |  |  |
|  |  |  |
|  |  |  |
|  |  |  |
|  |  |  |
|  |  |  |
|  |  |  |
|  |  |  |
|  |  |  |
|  |  |  |
|  |  |  |
|  |  |  |
|  |  |  |

| Reading Phonics | Reading Comprehension | Concepts About Print |
|---|---|---|
| | | |
| | | |
| | | |
| | | |
| | | |
| | | |
| | | |
| | | |
| | | |
| | | |
| | | |
| | | |
| | | |
| | | **Listening & Speaking** |
| | | |
| | | |
| | | |
| | | |
| | | |
| **Reference Skills** | **Reading Strategies** | |
| | | |
| | | |
| | | |
| | | |
| | | |
| | | |
| | | |
| | | |
| | | |
| | | |

©Teacher Jeanette Kinder Kollege

| Writing | Building Sentences | Grammar |
|---|---|---|
| | | |
| | | |
| | | |
| | | |
| | | |
| | | |
| **Informational Writing** | | |
| | | |
| | | |
| | | |
| | | |
| | | |
| | | |
| | | |
| | | |
| | | |
| | | |
| **Persuasive Writing** | **Writing a story** | **Composition** |
| | | |
| | | |
| | | |
| | | |
| | | |
| | | |
| | | |
| | | |
| | | |
| | | |
| | | |
| | | |
| | | |
| | | |

©Teacher Jeanette Kinder Kollege

| Science | Earth Science | Physical Science |
|---|---|---|
| | | |
| | | |
| | | |
| | | |
| | | |
| | | |
| Life Science | Energy Science | Healthy Habits |
| | | |
| | | |
| | | |
| | | |
| | | Physical Education |
| | | |
| | | |
| Social Studies | | |
| Map and Globe | Personal Finance | Our Nation |
| | | |
| | | |
| | | |
| | | |
| | | |
| | Good citizenship | |
| | | |
| | | |
| Current Events | | |
| | | |
| | | |
| | | |

©Teacher Jeanette Kinder Kollege

| | | |
|---|---|---|
| Math Process Skills | Numbers and Operations | |
| | | |
| | | |
| | | |
| | | |
| | | |
| | | |
| | | |
| | | |
| | | |
| | Geometry | Measurement |
| | | |
| Algebra | | |
| | | |
| | | |
| | | |
| | | |
| | | Electives |
| | | |
| | | |
| | | |
| | | |
| | | |
| | | |
| Technology | Computer Skills | Research Skills |
| | | |
| | | |
| | | |
| | | |
| | | |

©Teacher Jeanette Kinder Kollege

## 5-Step Lesson Plan

| Anticipatory Set | - Engage students.<br>- Connect with prior learning.<br>- Explain what students will learn.<br>- Explain what students will do.<br>- Connect to future learning. |
|---|---|
| Introduction of New Material | - Provide direct instruction of content.<br>- Model new skills.<br>- Check for understanding. |
| Guided Practice | - Facilitate student work. |
| Independent Practice | - Assign independent classwork or homework. |
| Closure | - Have students briefly summarize their learning. |

## Weekly Lesson Plan

| Subject | Mon | Tue | Wed | Thur | Fri |
|---|---|---|---|---|---|
| Character Education | | | | | |
| Math | | | | | |
| Language Arts Reading | | | | | |
| Science | | | | | |
| Social Studies | | | | | |
| Technology | | | | | |
| Language Arts Writing | | | | | |
| Language Art Spelling | | | | | |
| Electives | | | | | |

©Teacher Jeanette Kinder Kollege

# Weekly Report

| Name: | | Date: |
|---|---|---|
| Writing Skills | ○ Excellent<br>○ Satisfactory<br>○ Moderate<br>○ Needs Help | Notes: |
| Spelling Skills | ○ Excellent<br>○ Satisfactory<br>○ Moderate<br>○ Needs Help | Notes: |
| Reading Skills | ○ Excellent<br>○ Satisfactory<br>○ Moderate<br>○ Needs Help | Notes: |
| Math Skills | ○ Excellent<br>○ Satisfactory<br>○ Moderate<br>○ Needs Help | Notes: |
| Social Studies Skills | ○ Excellent<br>○ Satisfactory<br>○ Moderate<br>○ Needs Help | Notes: |
| Science Skills | ○ Excellent<br>○ Satisfactory<br>○ Moderate<br>○ Needs Help | Notes: |

©Teacher Jeanette Kinder Kollege

| Name: | | | Date: | |
|---|---|---|---|---|
| Computer Skills | ○ | Excellent | Notes: | |
| | ○ | Satisfactory | | |
| | ○ | Moderate | | |
| | ○ | Needs Help | | |
| Behavior Skills | ○ | Excellent | Notes: | |
| | ○ | Satisfactory | | |
| | ○ | Moderate | | |
| | ○ | Needs Help | | |
| Homework | ○ | Turns in homework | Notes: | |
| | ○ | Sometimes turns in | | |
| | ○ | Does not turn in | | |

## Next Week's Activities

| Monday | Tuesday | Wednesday | Thursday | Friday |
|---|---|---|---|---|
| | | | | |

©Teacher Jeanette Kinder Kollege

## Monthly Report

| Name: | | | Date: |
|---|---|---|---|
| Writing Skills | ○<br>○<br>○<br>○ | **Excellent**<br>**Satisfactory**<br>**Moderate**<br>**Needs Help** | Notes: |
| Spelling Skills | ○<br>○<br>○<br>○ | **Excellent**<br>**Satisfactory**<br>**Moderate**<br>**Needs Help** | Notes: |
| Reading Skills | ○<br>○<br>○<br>○ | **Excellent**<br>**Satisfactory**<br>**Moderate**<br>**Needs Help** | Notes: |
| Math Skills | ○<br>○<br>○<br>○ | **Excellent**<br>**Satisfactory**<br>**Moderate**<br>**Needs Help** | Notes: |
| Social Studies Skills | ○<br>○<br>○<br>○ | **Excellent**<br>**Satisfactory**<br>**Moderate**<br>**Needs Help** | Notes: |
| Science Skills | ○<br>○<br>○<br>○ | **Excellent**<br>**Satisfactory**<br>**Moderate**<br>**Needs Help** | Notes: |

©Teacher Jeanette Kinder Kollege

| Name: | | | Date: |
|---|---|---|---|
| Computer Skills | ○<br>○<br>○<br>○ | Excellent<br>Satisfactory<br>Moderate<br>Needs Help | Notes: |
| Behavior Skills | ○<br>○<br>○<br>○ | Excellent<br>Satisfactory<br>Moderate<br>Needs Help | Notes: |
| Homework | ○<br>○<br>○ | Turns in homework<br>Sometimes turns in<br>Does not turn in | Notes: |

## Next Month's Activities

| Monday | Tuesday | Wednesday | Thursday | Friday |
|---|---|---|---|---|
|  |  |  |  |  |

©Teacher Jeanette Kinder Kollege

# Substitute's Information

| Daily Procedures | | | |
|---|---|---|---|
| **Opening:** | | **Noon:** | |
| | | | |
| | | | |
| **Recess:** | | **Dismissal:** | |
| | | | |
| | | | |
| **Emergency Procedures** | | | |
| **Nurse's Schedule:** | | **Fire Drill:** | |
| | | | |
| | | | |
| **First Aid:** | | **Storm Drill:** | |
| | | | |
| | | | |
| **Special Health Information** | | | |
| | | **Notes:** | |
| | | | |
| | | | |
| | | | |
| | | | |
| | | | |
| | | | |
| **Students With Special Needs** | | | |
| | | | |
| | | | |
| | | | |
| **Note for Substitute Teacher** | | | |
| | | | |
| | | | |
| | | | |

©Teacher Jeanette Kinder Kollege

## Intervention Log

| Student's Name Area of Concern | Intervention being used for concern and frequency | Started | Result of Intervention |
|---|---|---|---|
| | | | |
| | | | |
| | | | |
| | | | |
| | | | |
| | | | |
| | | | |
| | | | |
| | | | |
| | | | |
| | | | |
| | | | |
| | | | |
| | | | |
| | | | |
| | | | |
| | | | |
| | | | |

©Teacher Jeanette Kinder Kollege

# Language Arts - Guided Writing

The Alphabet
- Begin with the Alphabet
- Use pictures to spell words

What do writers write?
- Building Sentences
- Punctuation, using period, question mark, comma, exclamation point, quotation marks, and apostrophe
- Rules for Capital Letters, beginning of a sentence, the word, I, names of people, places, pets, days of the week, months of the year,
- Noun
- Pronouns
- Personal Pronouns
- Build a Sentence
- I can build a sentence

Fix it Up!
- Rewrite sentence correctly
- Begin each sentence with a capital letter
- Add correct ending punctuation

My sentences have swag!
- S – starts with a capital.
- W – written neatly.
- A – a space between words.
- G – given punctuation.

Parts of a Story
- How a story is written
- The author writes the story
- The illustrator draws the pictures
- The title is the name of the book
- The setting is where the story takes place

- The characters are the people or animals in the story
- The plot is the events in the story: beginning, middle, and end.
- The conflict is the problems that the characters face
- The resolution is the part when the problem is solved.

Persuasive Writing - Opinions
- Begin to use formats appropriate to the genre (letter and poster)
- State an opinion
- Use words, illustrations, or graphics to support an opinion
- Something I think or feel
- I can use opinion words!
- What's your opinion?
- Sharing opinions with a friend

Making a List
- Putting a series of items written, mentioned, or considered, one following another
- School supply list
- Clothing list
- Shopping list
- Toy list

Label
- To put a word or words on something to identify
- I can label a picture!

Letter
- Written communication you send through the mail
- I can write a letter!
- What is at the post office?
- Where is the Post Office?

Adjectives
- Describing words
- Describes an object, food, person, or animal
- Tell us color, feel, sound, amount, behavior, size, food,

Sequencing
- First, next, last
- First, second, third, last.
- I can sequence events in a story

Narrative - Writing a story
- Write a story that involves one event
- Use drawings, letters, and phonetically spelled words to describe a
- Personal experience
- Write about a picture
- Write a story

Accessing Information
- Media center
- The library is one type of media center
- Media Purpose – to inform, entertain, or persuade
- Persuade (to get people to believe something or do what they are saying), inform (to give people more information or teach them about something) and entertain (keep people attention, usually in an enjoyable way)
- Digital Media

Writing Informational
- What writers do to influence people
- Write a piece that involves one topic
- Use drawings, letters, and phonetically spelled words to share information
- Publish a final copy
- Print Media
- Research

Grammar, Usage, Mechanics, and Spelling
- Use left to right and top to bottom directionality in writing
- Begin to use capitalization at the beginning of sentences and punctuation (periods and question marks) at the end of sentences
- Writing Across Genres

- Write or dictate to describe familiar persons, places, objects, or experiences explore prewriting, drafting, revising, editing, and publishing
- Write legibly in manuscript own first and last names with initial capital letters, self-selected and teacher-selected words, and upper and lower case letters of the alphabet
- Begin to develop a draft from pre-writing
- Begin to develop a sense of closure
- Begin to use describing words
- Pre-write orally or in writing to generate ideas (graphic organizers and pictures)

Response to Literature
- Retell a story orally, through pictures, or in writing
- Make connections: text-to-self, text-to-text, text-to-word

Accessing Information / Reference Skills
- Explore the use of the media center, picture books, audiovisual resources, and available technology for reading and writings

Good Citizenship
- Community is a place where people live
- Community Helpers are people in the community who help others
- How do community helpers help? A police officer keeps us safe, a teacher helps us learn, and a doctor helps us feel better, a market woman sells us food
- A good citizen is also a community helper
- What I want to be when I grow up

# Writing Rating Scale

Using the rubric scale to read: N=Never, S=Sometimes, A=Always

| Writing Rubric | N | S | A |
|---|---|---|---|
| My illustration matches my story | | | |
| I wrote reasons to support my topic | | | |
| My writing is on topic | | | |
| I used correct punctuation | | | |
| My handwriting is neat and I use finger spaces | | | |
| My sentences make sense | | | |
| I started my sentences with capital letters | | | |
| I stated my opinion | | | |
| I wrote reasons to support my opinion | | | |
| | | | |
| **Overall Score** | | | |

# A Writer's Eye

Do you have a writer's eye?

I see a **capital letter** at the beinning of my sentence.
The dog ran.

I see finger spaces between words.

The dog ran.

I see **lowercase** letters throughout my sentence.
The dog ran.

I see **punctuation** at the end of my sentence.
The dog ran.

# Types of Sentences

There are four types of sentences. Each type of sentence serves a different purpose and has o specific type of punctuation mark.

| Declarative . | A declarative sentence tells a statement. It ends in a period. **It is a bright and sunny day.** |
|---|---|
| Imperative . ! | An imperative sentence gives a command. It can end with a period or exclamation mark. **Take the trash out. STOP!** |
| Interrogative ? | An interrogative sentence asks a question. It ends in a question mark. **Are you going to the game tonight?** |
| Exclamatory ! | A exclamatory sentence is a statement that shows emotion. It ends in an exclamation mark. **Wow! You won!** |

## Punctuation

Punctuation - ending marks.
1. Use a period (.) when making a statement.
2. Use a question mark (?) when asking a question.
3. Use a comma (,) when separating single words in a series {making a list} and when writing the date.
4. Use an exclamation point (!) when you're: *Excited, *Demanding, and *Exaggerating.
5. Use quotation marks when: (") *A character is speaking in a story.
6. Use an apostrophe (') when you're *making a contraction, or *showing possession.

# Rules for Capital Letters

1. Beginning of a Sentence.
2. The Word ' I '
3. Names of. . . People, Places, Pets
4. Calendar

| Days of the Week | Months | Holidays |
|---|---|---|
| Sunday<br>Monday<br>Tuesday<br>Wednesday<br>Thursday<br>Friday<br>Saturday | January<br>February<br>March<br>April<br>May<br>June<br>July<br>August<br>September<br>October<br>November<br>December | Thanksgiving<br>Christmas<br>New Year's Day |

| Nouns | Pronouns | Personal Pronouns | |
|---|---|---|---|
| Noun is a person, an animal, a place, or a thing. | I<br>me<br>he<br>it<br>she<br>we<br>you<br>they | I am<br>you are<br>he is<br>she is<br>it is<br>we are<br>you are<br>they are | I'm<br>you're<br>he's<br>she's<br>it's<br>we're<br>you're<br>they're |

# Basic Sentence Structure

Starts with a capital.
Written neatly.
A space between words.
Given punctuation.

Go over these sentences for Basic Sentence Structure.

I am little.
You are big.
He is tall.
She is happy.
It is brown.
We are going to school.
They are coming tomorrow.

Have student build sentences with these "sentence starters".

| | | |
|---|---|---|
| I see a | Look at my | I have seen |
| I saw a | Here is the | I can see the |
| I see the | I have a | Here is the big |
| I like the | It is a | It is an |
| I like my | Here is an | I like to see |
| This is my | I can see a | |
| This is a | I love the | |
| Look at the | I saw the | |

## Verbs Show Actions

| | |
|---|---|
| push | slide |
| sit | hang |
| jump | pull |
| slide | swing |
| bounce | ride |

Discuss action words for each playground equipment and daily activities at home.

# Adjectives

Descriptive Words That Tell Us . . .

| Color | Feel | Sound | Amount |
|---|---|---|---|
| red<br>brown<br>green<br>blue<br>tan | rough<br>soft<br>hot<br>furry<br>smooth | loud<br>quiet | full<br>empty |
| **Behavior** | | **Food** | **Size** |
| wild<br>silly<br>crazy<br>happy<br>funny | excited<br>sad<br>hurt<br>upset<br>angry | sour<br>salty<br>sweet<br>cold | huge<br>tiny<br>small<br>tall |
| **Adjectives describe an object, food, person, or animal.** | | | |
| heavy<br>light<br>thick<br>thin<br>young<br>wet | old<br>straight<br>narrow<br>dirty<br>clean<br>smelly | | |

# Sequencing

The order in which things are or connect.

| 1 | 2 | 3 | 4 |
|---|---|---|---|
| First, | Next, | Last. | |
| First, | Second, | Third, | Last. |
| | | | |

## It's Raining

| 1 | 2 | 3 |
|---|---|---|
| First, | Next, | Last. |

## Time for Bed

| First, | Second, | Third, | Last. |
|---|---|---|---|
| 1 | 2 | 3 | 4 |

**Practical**

**Discuss the sequence in each story.**

A Chick Grows Up
It's Lunch Time
My Birthday Cake
Washing My Hands
When I Wake Up
My Tomato Garden
Planting a Flower

# How a Book is Made

1. The author writes the story.
2. The illustrator draws the pictures.
3. The title is the name of the book.
4. The setting is where the story takes place.
5. The characters are the people or animals in the story.
6. The plot is the events in the story; beginning, middle and end.
7. The conflict is the problem that the characters face.
8. The resolution is the part when the problem is solved.

# The Writing Process

Writing is a process. Strong writers don't publish the very first thing they put down on the paper. They go through several steps to make sure they are doing their very best writing.

## There are 5 steps in the writing process.

| Step 1: Brainstorming | During this step, writers think about all the ideas they have for their writing. They might use a web or graphic organizer to jot down their ideas. |
|---|---|
| Step 2: Drafting | During this step, writers start to write with their final piece in mind. They begin writing their ideas in order. |
| Step 3: Revising | During this step, writers reread what they have written. They might add some details or change the order of things. |
| Step 4: Editing | During this step, writers check their writing for any mechanical errors they might have made. It's their final check. |
| Step 5: Publishing | During this step, writers rewrite their piece one final time to share it with their readers. |

# Opinion Writing

## Facts & Opinions

Many times, authors will include facts and opinions in their writing. It is important to know the difference between them.

| Facts | Opinions |
|---|---|
| A fact is a statsment that can be proven to be true or false. | An opinion is a personal belief Or feeling. An opinion cannot be proven. |
| Authors (writers) include facts and opinions in their writing to help influence the reader. ||
| Facts: | Thanksgiving is in the month of November.<br><br>Ask Yourself: Can this be proven? |
| Opinions: | Thanksgiving is the best holiday.<br><br>Ask Yourself: Could people disagree? |

 Have students make a list of things they like and things they do not like. Then, have them use opinion words to tell what they think and how they feel about them.

## Sentence Starters

| | |
|---|---|
| I think | I feel |
| I believe | In my opinion |
| My favorite | I like |
| The best thing about | I do not like |
| If I had | I agree |
| I prefer | I disagree |
| I know | You will love |

## Transition Words

| | |
|---|---|
| First | Also |
| Second | Another reason |
| Third | Finally |
| Next | Last |

## Writing the Conclusion

| | |
|---|---|
| All in all | That is why I believe |
| In conclusion | As you can see |
| To summarize | It is clear that |

# Writing a Letter

A letter is a written or printed communication one sends through the mail. (post office)

Have students write 2 letters; one to a friend and one to a parent.

☐ I have words. dog

☐ I have spaces.

☐ I have punctuation. .?!

☐ My colors make sense.

**Write a Letter**

Dear Mama, ← Who is it to?
I like school. We have a lot of fun. My teacher reads to us. We listen to books with our headphones on. It is like watching TV without pictures. It is fun too. I sit with my friend, Musu, at lunch. Musu's favorite thing to do at recess is jump rope. I like it too. ← What you want to say.

Zaq ← Your name.

# The Post Office

The post office is a place where mail is received, handled, and sent out. The post office is another connection to the world. The post office can send your letter to anyone in Liberia, or to another country.

Where is the Post Office? Plan a trip to your local post office or set up a Post Office in a dramatic play.

## How to mail a letter.

First,
I write
my letter.

Second,
I put the
letter in an
envelope and
address it.

Third,
I put a
stamp
on the
envelope.

Last,
I take the
letter to
the post
office.

What is at the Post Office?

letters

stamps

envelopes

packages

# Language Arts - Guided Spelling

The Alphabet
- Writing and Spelling begin with the Alphabet.
- UPPER CASE
- lower case
- Spell and write First Name
- Spell and write Last Name

Spelling Words I
- 2-Letter Words
- Building words using Pyramids
- Build 2-Letter
- Word Pyramids
- 3-Letter Words

Alphabetical Order
- Arrange words in the order of the letters of the alphabet
- Alphabetize lists, words

Rhyming
- Maze Rhymes
- Rhyme and Reason
- Perfect Pairs
- Rhyming Time!
- Odd Rhyme Out
- Perfect Pairs Too
- Word Search Puzzle

Spelling Words II
- 4-letter Words
- Rhyming Butterflies
- Build-a-Word

- Odd One Out
- 5-letter words

Spelling Words III
- 6-letter words
- Trace your 7-letter words
- 7-letter Pyramids
- Trace your 8-letter words

Word Lists
Let's write some Christmas words
Number Words
Color Words
My Color Words
Patriotic Words
Rainy Season
Social Relations
Fruits & Vegetables
Here Are Some Nuts!
Things at the Beach
Weather Words
Body Parts
Opposite
Clothing Words
Let's Eat
Months of the Year
7 Days a Week!
School Days
Write your school supply list
Graduation Words

Word Smart Puzzles
Animals at the Zoo
Animals in the water
Animals on the Farm
Bugs & Insects
Pets
Food
Fruits and Veggies
Transportation
School Things
Going Shopping
How Do You Feel Today?
I Love My Family
Family Words

## 2-Letter Words

| | |
|---|---|
| am | to |
| or | by |
| as | us |
| of | we |
| at | Mr. |
| be | Dr. |
| go | Ms. |
| me | TV |
| he | |
| up | |
| hi | |
| if | |
| an | |
| my | |
| is | |
| ax | |
| it | |
| no | |
| on | |
| do | |
| in | |
| ox | |
| so | |

## 3-Letter Words

| | | |
|---|---|---|
| eat | out | did |
| act | cry | all |
| air | wax | eel |
| any | rob | end |
| ate | job | fad |
| his | Mrs. | ape |
| bad | fan | are |
| ban | has | art |
| bat | nap | ask |
| bay | six | fed |
| bed | sky | fit |
| bee | low | fly |
| pat | off | for |
| top | our | fur |
| get | pal | gap |
| two | pay | got |
| use | pop | gun |
| pad | pot | her |
| cap | boo | hey |
| him | bug | hit |
| car | buy | how |
| see | cab | its |
| hot | can | jar |
| pin | cub | kid |

| lad | may | leg | gum | add |
| --- | --- | --- | --- | --- |
| lap | dot | now | key | let |
| led | lit | red | arm | mug |
| lot | toe | bus | toy | hat |
| put | pan | eye | jam | big |
| ran | new | win | mat | nut |
| rat | hay | zoo | hog | boy |
| rip | yea | jet | cat | box |
| run | tap | man | why | ram |
| saw | set | pie | cut | hug |
| sea | ant | sad | mad | shy |
| she | say | yes | wet | ham |
| sit | wed | ice | but | dog |
| son | one | cow | log | bet |
| sun | and | oil | pig | |
| tag | cup | try | hut | |
| taz | dam | fun | fox | |
| the | had | | | |
| was | day | | | |
| way | van | | | |
| who | row | | | |
| owl | ten | | | |
| few | hen | | | |
| zip | | | | |
| you | | | | |
| old | | | | |
| egg | | | | |
| not | | | | |

**When trying to spell a word,**

1. Say the word slowly.
2. Stretch the word. Count the sounds.
3. Draw a line for each sound.
4. Write letter(s) for each sound.
5. CHECK IT! Run your finger under it and blend. Does it sound right? Does it look right?

Practical

56

## 4-Letter Words

| | | | | |
|---|---|---|---|---|
| | | they | gave | mall |
| | | this | gift | wall |
| also | open | week | gold | ball |
| away | over | went | grow | fall |
| baby | play | were | hair | talk |
| back | read | will | hand | walk |
| barn | rent | wish | hard | good |
| bead | ride | word | have | food |
| bear | rule | work | head | book |
| been | safe | worm | hear | look |
| beep | said | yard | hers | tell |
| bend | seal | your | high | sell |
| bent | send | duck | hill | well |
| best | shoe | easy | hole | bell |
| come | sick | ever | hope | cake |
| cost | side | face | hurt | take |
| crab | soft | farm | jump | bake |
| dark | some | feel | keep | down |
| drop | song | fill | kind | town |
| lion | soon | find | kite | bull |
| lose | star | fire | king | pull |
| loss | stop | fish | ring | full |
| more | sure | foot | five | name |
| move | tend | four | live | same |
| neat | than | free | miss | help |
| next | that | frog | kiss | calf |
| nine | them | from | call | here |
| only | then | game | tall | love |

## 5-Letter Words

| | | | | |
|---|---|---|---|---|
| made | road | about | brown | party |
| many | room | above | camel | plate |
| both | cold | after | candy | price |
| came | colt | small | carry | round |
| used | last | stick | clean | seven |
| very | late | store | color | sheep |
| wait | lend | story | count | skunk |
| told | yell | swim | daddy | |
| girl | zero | table | dream | |
| give | what | these | dress | |
| glad | when | thing | eight | |
| goat | light | three | every | |
| tree | like | tiger | fight | |
| true | line | train | floor | |
| want | deer | tried | ghost | |
| wave | doll | white | goose | |
| lost | bird | witch | grass | |
| meow | blue | woman | green | |
| pole | xray | write | heart | |
| poor | boss | zebra | hello | |
| with | care | alone | house | |
| boat | palm | apple | large | |
| wolf | sent | beach | moose | |
| meet | pass | begin | music | |
| lamb | door | black | nurse | |
| land | dove | bring | paper | |
| city | draw | | | |
| rice | rock | | | |

## 6-Letter Words

| | | 
|---|---|
| Africa | making |
| almost | monkey |
| always | mother |
| animal | number |
| answer | orange |
| before | people |
| better | please |
| church | purple |
| circle | rabbit |
| coming | friend |
| cookie | school |
| crayon | spider |
| donkey | sticky |
| Easter | strong |
| family | things |
| farmer | turtle |
| father | turkey |
| flower | yellow |
| splash | zipper |
| freely | peanut |
| garden | |
| golden | |
| health | |
| sister | |
| kitten | |
| little | |

## 7-Letter Words

address
rainbow
because
chicken
feeling
brother
fireman
giraffe
holiday
picture
present
pumpkin
tractor
Liberia

## 8-Letter Words

Children
umbrella
elephant
dinosaur
raindrop
goldfish
Monrovia
birthday

## 9-Letter Words

pineapple
Christmas

**When trying to spell a hard word,**

1. Say the word slowly.
2. Break the word into chunks.
3. Work one chunk at a time:
4. Use word parts you know.
5. Remember a vowel in each chunk.
6. CHECK IT! Run your finger under and blend the chunks. Does it sound right? Does it look right?

# Compound Words

A compound word is a combination of two or more words that form one new word.

Practical

Speak the first word of a compound word aloud. Instruct the students to say the word and clap. Then speak the second word of the compound aloud. Have the students repeat this word and clap. Then tell the students to say both words together and to clap for each word.

| applesauce | grasshopper | underwear |
| bathroom | haircut | watermelon |
| bedroom | inside | fireman |
| birthday | mailbox | doghouse |
| blueberry | outside | sunglasses |
| cupcake | playground | lipstick |
| downstairs | snowflake | pancake |
| firefly | toothbrush | fishbowl |
| goldfish | upstairs | football |

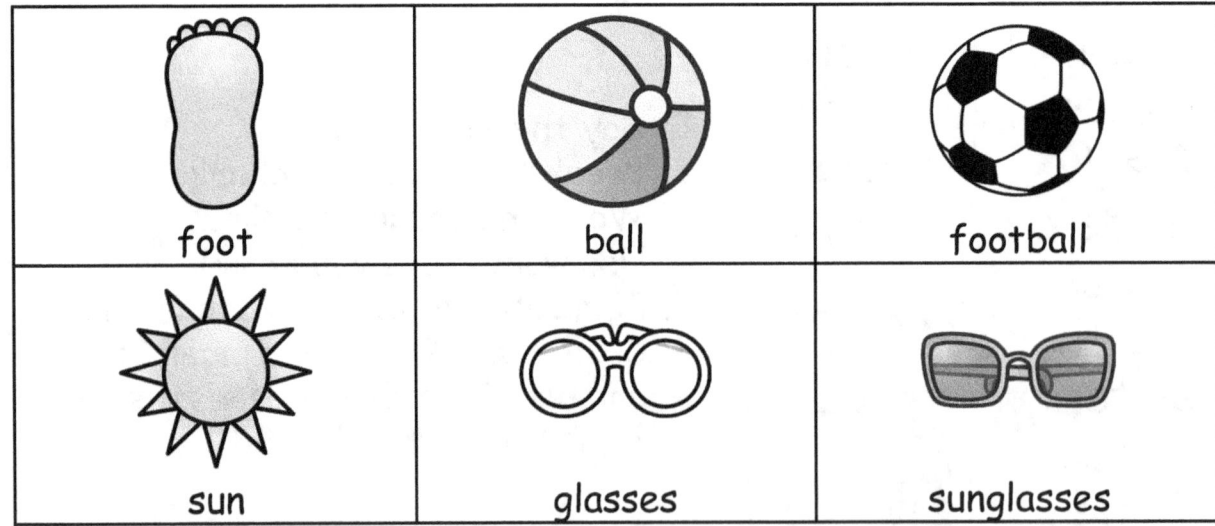

# Synonym Words

A synonym is a word that has the same or almost the same meaning as another word.

| | | |
|---|---|---|
| also - too | speak - talk | finish - end |
| happy - glad | rich - wealthy | start - begin |
| small - little | note - memo | trash - garbage |
| gift - present | fog - mist | |
| kind - nice | pig - hog | |
| finish - end | rescue - save | |
| journey - travel | fortunate - lucky | |
| lamp - light | equal - same | |
| money - cash | easy - simple | |
| midday - noon | soil - dirt | |

| | |
|---|---|
| big \| large | fast \| quick |
| start \| begin | present \| gift |
| pig \| hog | travel \| journey |

# Antonym Words

An antonym is a word that has the opposite meaning as another word.

big - small
loud - quiet
tall - short
wet - dry
above - below
back - front
black - white
clean - dirty
night - day

right way up-upside down
happy - sad
closed - open
inside - outside
full - empty
happy - sad
high - low
hot - cold
hard - soft

under - above
awake - asleep
old - young
light - heavy

# Language Arts – Guided Reading

Listening, Speaking, and Viewing
- Listen attentively to respond to questions and to follow two-part directions
- Participate in vocal speaking and creative drama
- Recite short poems, rhymes, songs, and stories with repeated patterns
- Use oral language to relate experiences and expand vocabulary
- Recall orally a series of three visually presented items
- Listen and speak appropriately with peers and adults
- Repeat auditory sequences: letters, words, numbers, and rhythmic patterns
- Communicate effectively when using descriptive language, relating experiences, and retelling stories
- Describe people, places, things, locations, and actions
- Use complete sentences when speaking and begin to use subject-verb agreement and tense correctly

Reading Strategies and Comprehension
- Listen to, select, and read a variety of literary (e.g., short stories and poems) and informational texts and materials for pleasure and to gain knowledge, tell stories using wordless picture books and picture sequences
- Make predictions from pictures and titles
- Discriminate between real and imaginary content in texts
- Explore the comparison and contrast of content within stories
- Retell stories and respond to literal, inferential, and evaluative questions about the story
- Retell and identify the beginning, middle, and end of stories
- Sequence events in a story
- Demonstrate that print makes sense by reading and explaining one's own writings and drawings

- Ask and answer questions about essential narrative elements (e.g., beginning-middle-end, setting, characters, problems, events, resolution) of a read-aloud text
- Use prior knowledge, graphic features (illustrations), and graphic organizers to understand text
- S-O "SO" reading song

Concepts About Print
- Relate written language to spoken language
- Distinguish among written letters, words, and sentences
- Recognize that sentences in print are made up of separate words
- Segment phonemes in high-frequency words
- Blend phonemes to make high-frequency words
- Identify and match all upper and lower case letters of the alphabet out of sequence
- Recognize common environmental print such as common signs and logos and recognize that print and pictures (signs and labels, newspapers, and informational books) can inform, entertain, and persuade
- Demonstrate principles of directionality by holding print materials in the correct position and using left-to-right and top-to-bottom progression
- Begin to recognize and understand that punctuation and capitalization are used in all written sentences

Word Work/Vocabulary/Phonics/Fluency
- Listen to a variety of texts and use new vocabulary in oral language
- Recognize words in a familiar context
- Identify own first and last name in print
- Read first 50 high-frequency sight words and common words, such as colors, numbers, names, and places
- Recognize and produce rhyming and non-rhyming words
- Recognize simple word opposites
- Match all consonant and short-vowel sounds to appropriate letters
- Identify component sounds (phonemes and combinations of phonemes) in spoken words
- Blend and segment syllables in spoken words

- Blend sounds to read one-syllable words
- Read previously taught high-frequency words at the rate of 30 words correct per minute
- Read previously taught grade-level text with appropriate expression
- Apply learned phonics skills when reading words and sentences in stories
- Use words that signal sequence relationships such as first, next, and last
- Explore the use of a Pictionary or dictionary to identify words
- Discuss the meaning of words and understand that some words have multiple meanings
- Connect life experiences to the read-aloud text

Accessing Information / Reference Skills
- Explore the use of the media center, picture books, audiovisual resources, and available technology for reading and writings
- Audiobook - when children listen to audiobooks, they hear firsthand the proper pacing and intonations of reading, how punctuation should sound, and how reading should sound.

# What is Reading?

Reading is understanding the story. Reading is fun. Reading helps you find stuff you didn't know. Are you Ready to Read?

## Let's Learn to Read!

Know your alphabet,
Know your spelling,
Know beginning sounds,
know ending sounds, and
Know punctuation.

## These are letters.

| A a | I i | H h | T t |
|-----|-----|-----|-----|
| C c | E e | K k | L l |

### These are words.

| cat | the | like | I |
|-----|-----|------|---|
| see | my  | ate  | am |

### This is a sentence.

I like the cat.

I see a big hen.

Practical — Students must first complete the alphabet exercises in their Language Arts Reading workbook from page 14 to page 39.

## Beginning Sounds

For students who are getting ready to read, they need help practicing beginning sounds for each letter of the alphabet. Help them master letter recognition and letter sounds of the alphabet. Building this relationship is a critical step in setting the foundation for learning to read and write.

**Identify the initial or beginning sound of each word/picture.**

| | |
|---|---|
| **A** is for ant.<br>The **a** says /a/ like **ant,** ( apple, ax) | |
| **B** is for ball.<br>The **b** says /b/ like **ball,** ( bat, bed, boat, bike) | |
| **C** is for cat.<br>The **c** says /c/ like **cat,** ( car, cow, cup, can) | |
| **D** is for dog.<br>The **d** says /d/ like **dog,** ( duck, doll, dip, desk) | |
| **E** is for egg.<br>The **e** says /e/ like **egg,** ( elephant, elf, envelope) | |
| **F** is for fan.<br>The **f** says /f/ like **fan,** ( fox, farm, fish, fire) | |

| | |
|---|---|
| **G** is for girl. <br> The **g** says /g/ like **girl,** (gift, girl, gum, game) | |
| **H** is for hat. <br> The **h** says /h/ like **hat,** ( house, hand, hug) | |
| **I** is for inch. <br> The **i** says /i/ like **inch,** ( igloo, iguana, instruments) | |
| **J** is for jar. <br> The **j** says /j/ like **jar,** ( jam, jacket, jet, jail) | |
| **K** is for key. <br> The **k** says /k/ like **key,** ( king, kiss, kettle) | |
| **L** is for log. <br> The **l** says /l/ like **log,** ( lamp, leaf, lip, lock) | |
| **M** is for men. <br> The **m** says /m/ like **men,** ( mug, map, mail, mice ) | |
| **N** is for nut. <br> The **n** says /n/ like **nut,** ( nose, net, nest ) | |
| **O** is for ox. <br> The **o** says /o/ like **ox,** ( olive, office, otter) | |
| **P** is for pan. <br> The **p** says /p/ like **pan,** ( pen, pot, purse, pillow) | |
| **Q** is for queen. <br> The **q** says /q/ like **queen,** ( quilt, quiet, quiz) | |
| **R** is for rat. <br> The **r** says /r/ like **rat,** ( road, rope, ring ) | |

| | |
|---|---|
| **S** is for sun. <br> The **s** says /s/ like **sun,** ( sock, sun, seven, saw, seed) | |
| **T** is for tub. <br> The **t** says /t/ like **tub,** ( turtle, tea, tooth) | |
| **U** is for umbrella. <br> The **u** says /u/ like **umbrella,** ( upstairs, under, upload) | |
| **V** is for van. <br> The **v** says /v/ like **van,** ( vest, valcano, vet) | |
| **W** is for web. <br> The **w** says /w/ like **web,** ( wet, watch, wolf) | |
| **X** is for box. <br> The **x** says /x/ like **box,** ( fox, six. mix) | |
| **Y** is for yoyo. <br> The **y** says /y/ like **yoyo,** ( yarn, yard, yacht) | |
| **Z** is for zebra. <br> The **z** says /z/ like **zebra,** ( zipper, zoo, zero, **zebra**) | |

# Short Vowel Sounds

Short **a** makes the sound of a in

c a n     h a t     m a t

Short **e** makes the sound of e in

h e n     n e st     e gg

Short **i** makes the sound of i in

w i g     p i g     f i sh

Short **o** makes the sound of o in

fr o g     l o g     p o nd

Short **u** makes the sound of u in

b u s     c u p     s u n

| | a t | a n | a m | a g | a d | a p |
|---|---|---|---|---|---|---|
| **a** | hat<br>cat<br>cat | van<br>can<br>fan | ram<br>jam<br>yam | rag<br>bag<br>tag | mad<br>sad<br>pad | map<br>cap<br>nap |
| | e n | e d | e t | e g | | |
| **e** | pen<br>ten<br>hen | bed<br>wed<br>red | wet<br>net<br>jet | peg<br>beg<br>leg | | |
| | i t | i n | i p | i g | | |
| **i** | hit<br>sit<br>kit | pin<br>bin<br>fin | lip<br>zip<br>dip | pig<br>wig<br>dig | | |
| | o p | o t | o b | o g | | |
| **o** | mop<br>pop<br>top | hot<br>pot<br>dot | cob<br>sob<br>rob | hog<br>dog<br>log | | |
| | u g | u t | u n | u b | u d | |
| **u** | rug<br>mug<br>jug | hut<br>cut<br>nut | sun<br>bun<br>run | cub<br>tub | mud<br>bud | |

# Ending Sounds
## b, d, f, l, r, x, s, p, m, g, n

owl  fox  tub  leaf

bear  bug  pig  sun

bird  bus  stop  drum

book  box  milk  dog

# My Sounds Chart

| | | | | |
|---|---|---|---|---|
| **a** — c<u>a</u>t | **e** — h<u>e</u>n | **i** — p<u>i</u>g | **o** — f<u>o</u>x | **u** — s<u>u</u>n |
| **th** — <u>th</u>umb | **ch** — <u>ch</u>icken | **sh** — <u>sh</u>ell | **wh** — <u>wh</u>istle | **qu** — <u>qu</u>een |
| **ar** — st<u>ar</u> | **or** — h<u>or</u>se | **er** — flow<u>er</u> | **ir** — b<u>ir</u>d | **ur** — p<u>ur</u>se |
| **ay** — h<u>ay</u> | **ai** — sn<u>ai</u>l | **ee** — b<u>ee</u> | **ea** — l<u>ea</u>f | **ea** — thr<u>ea</u>d |
| **oa** — b<u>oa</u>t | **ow** — b<u>ow</u>l | **ow** — c<u>ow</u> | **ou** — cl<u>ou</u>d | **oo** — igl<u>oo</u> |

# Phonics Sounds

| Sh- | Th- | Ch- | -unk |
|---|---|---|---|
| shark | the | chin | skunk |
| sheep | that | chomp | bunk |
| shop | they | chop | dunk |
| shut | this | chug | junk |
| she | thumb | chain | sunk |
| shoe | three | cheer | shrunk |
| ship | there | chief | stunk |
| shot | think | check | trunk |
| shell | thorn | chick | chipmunk |

| -ink | -ing | -ay | -ai |
|---|---|---|---|
| link | king | bay | snail |
| pink | sing | day | sail |
| sink | ring | may | nail |
| wink | wing | ray | pail |
| blink | ding | say | tail |
| drink | spring | way | paint |
| stink | sting | gray | braid |
| ink | swing | play | rain |
| think | string | tray | train |

## Sounds Phonics

| -ee | -ea | -oa | bossy E |
|---|---|---|---|
| bee | beak | road | whale |
| deer | read | toad | white |
| feet | peach | foal | snake |
| see | flea | roar | five |
| tree | squeak | boat | kite |
| queen | mean | coat | cone |
| green | beast | goat | cube |
| sheep | eat | goal | June |
| tweet | treat | soap | name |

| vowel walk | oo (as in boot) |
|---|---|
| blue | moo |
| glue | food |
| fruit | zoo |
| suit | roof |
| die | pool |
| pie | school |
| tie | broom |
| clue | spoon |
| cried | goose |

# My Blends Chart

| bl | cl | fl | gl | pl |
|---|---|---|---|---|
| blue | clown | fly | glove | plane |
| **sl** | **br** | **cr** | **dr** | **fr** |
| slide | branch | crab | drum | frog |
| **gr** | **pr** | **tr** | **wr** | **thr** |
| grapes | prize | tree | write | throw |
| **st** | **sp** | **sn** | **sc** | **sk** |
| star | spider | snail | scared | skate |
| **sm** | **sw** | **tw** | | |
| smile | swing | twins | | |

# Beginning Blends

**l blends**

cl
fl
gl
pl
sl

clown
flower
glue
plane
slide

**r blends**

br
cr
dr
fr
gr
tr

brush  frog
crayon  grape
drum  tree

**s blends**

sk
sl
sm
sn
sp
st

skate  snail
slide  spider
smile  stamp

**h digraphs**

ch
ph
sh
th
wh

cheese
phone
shoe
thumb
wheel

gift, hand, tent,
first, desk, swing

# Ending Blends and Digraphs

-ft   -nd   -nt   -st   -sk   -ing

# Write in the Blends

## br bl cr cl fl fr

**B Blends** 
- ____ocks 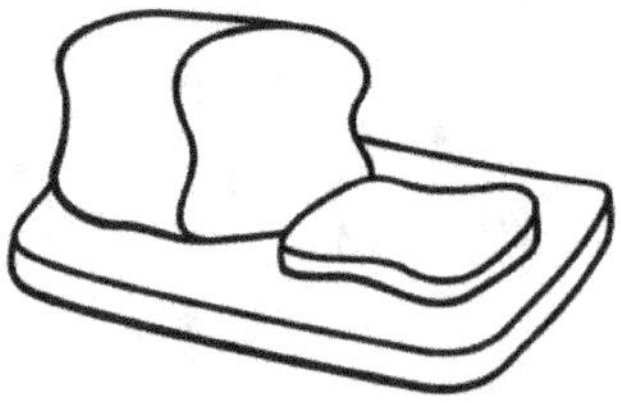
- ____ead 
- ____oom

**C Blends** 
- ____ab 
- ____ock 
- ____own

**F Blends** 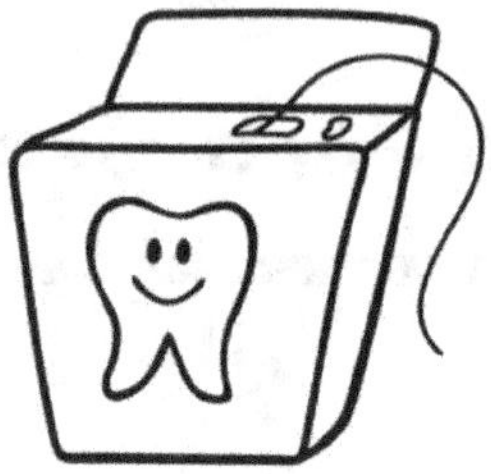
- ____oss 
- ____og 
- ____y

# Rhyming

Rhyme: close similarity in the final sounds of two or more words (to end with the same sound)

Phonemic Awareness provides a strong foundation for early reading success. As students become more proficient in hearing, identifying and manipulating sounds (phonemes), they can move onto segmenting and blending words. A systematic and cohesive approach to teaching phonological awareness can build confident readers who are less likely to struggle with decoding and spelling skills. Students with strong phonemic awareness are much more likely to be successful readers.

Learning how to rhyme is important to early reading success. Students learn how language works when they learn how to rhyme. Rhyming helps students notice work with sounds within different words. When children can confidently rhyme, they become better readers, spellers, and writers.

Write new rhyming words by adding letters to the beginning of:

**ap at en et in ip it op ug & ut**

Use the letters below.

# d, l, t, b, c, f, h, m, p, s, fl

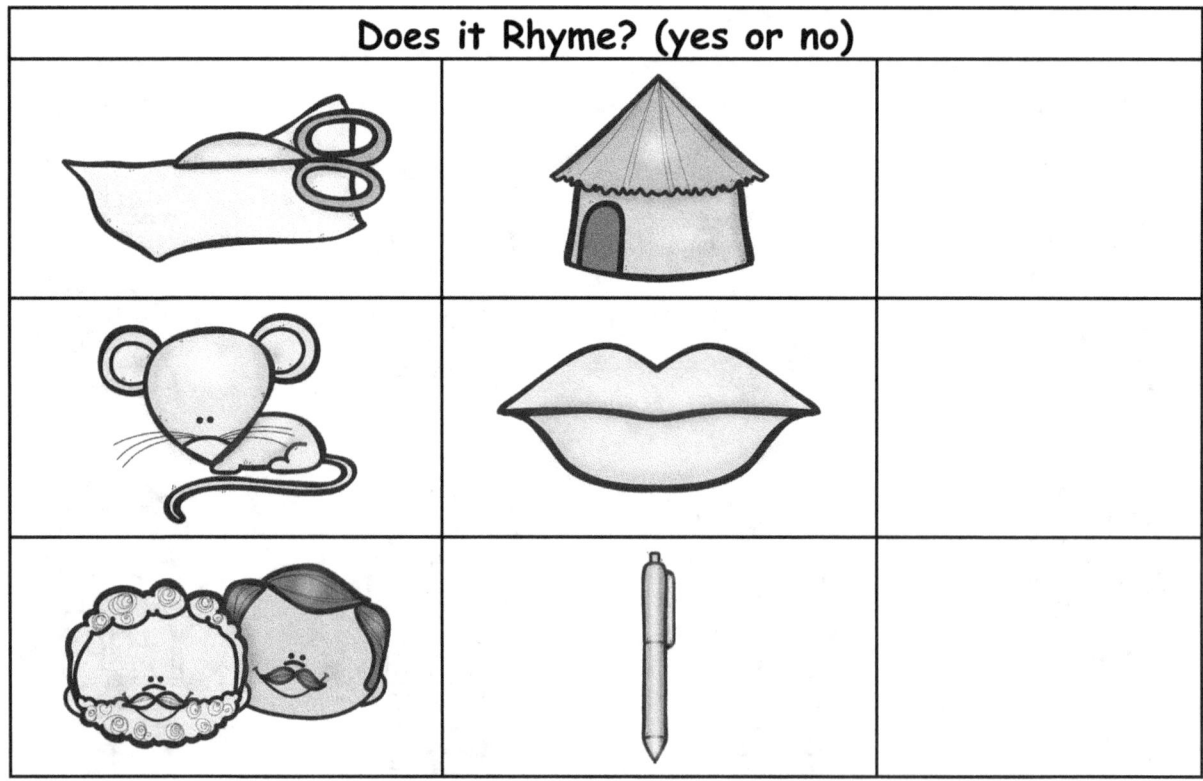

# Syllables

| 1-Syllable Words (1 claps) | 2-Syllable Words (2 claps) | 3-Syllable Words (3 claps) |
|---|---|---|
| jet<br>eye<br>ax<br>gate<br>leaf<br>bug<br>stop<br>name<br>gas<br>lamp<br>boat<br>gum | Christmas<br>table<br>picture<br>today<br>woman<br>table<br>zipper<br>puppy<br>zebra<br>baby<br>chicken | computer<br>butterfly<br>elephant<br>pineapple |

| Syllables Sorting ||
|---|---|
| Write the name of the picture in the correct box. ||
| 1 | 2 |
| 3 | 4 |

# Reading Fluency

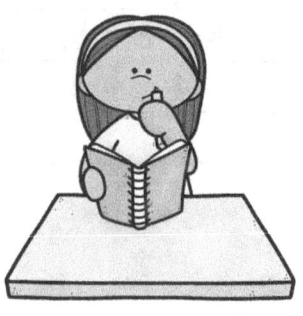

The kindergarten curriculum is designed to teach all children how to read. It is perfectly OK for people to enter kindergarten not reading. However, your child does need reading readiness skills. The goal is students must be able to read (with fluency) at the grade expectation words per minute rate, reads with expression, and recognizes punctuation within the text.

## What is Reading Fluency?

Reading fluency is the ability to read with speed, accuracy, and proper expression. Reading fluency is an essential element of reading instruction in K-2nd grade. Teach students to read with expression, to pay attention to punctuation, and to read with inflection in his voice. Better fluency leads to greater understanding.

### Ways to improve reading fluency

• Read aloud to children to provide a model of fluent reading. A regular read-aloud period is a must in any elementary classroom. No matter their age or ability, children need a frequent model of fluent reading.

• Have children listen and follow along with audio recordings. Teachers can record themselves as they read aloud to their class and use it later as an audio recording.

• Practice sight words using playful activities; when children know many words by sight, they're less likely to be awkward, choppy readers. A good goal is that children should master 20 sight words by the end of Kindergarten and 100 sight words by the end of First Grade.

• Let students perform a reader's theater. A Reader's theater requires no set or costumes and is a fantastic way to improve fluency. Children take turns reading their parts from a script and bring the text alive through their voices. To create a script, create an original play with speaking parts or adapt a familiar story (or book off VTP reading list) by typing it up into several speaking parts.

• Do the paired reading. Make paired reading (also called "buddy reading") a daily practice within their literacy block. To do a paired reading, put students in pairs and have them read to each other. Pair more fluent readers with less fluent readers, but be careful not to make the ability gap too great. Students can take turns reading by sentence, paragraph, or page. The teacher and student can take turns reading too.

• Try echo reading; with echo reading, the teacher displays an enlarged text so that students can follow along. This might be a Big Book or a text displayed on a blackboard. The teacher often points to words as she reads a sentence or short paragraph. Then she points to the words again as students echo her reading.

• Do choral reading; with choral reading, the teacher reads an enlarged text several times until students are familiar with it. Then the class joins her as they read the text together. Nursery rhymes, songs, and funny poems are fantastic for choral reading.

• Do the repeated reading. Echo reading and choral reading are both forms of repeated reading. Repeated reading is also something that students can do individually. Choose a short passage of 100-200 words and have students read the same passage multiple times. Have them time their reading and graph their results to see a visual record of improvement. A variation is to set a timer for 1-2 minutes and have students record how many words they read during each reading. Again, use a graph to chart progress.

• Practice "scooping" phrases. While we encourage beginning readers to point to each word as they read, this is something we want our readers to grow out of. Enter scooping phrases! Simply write a short passage on paper, then guide your learner as he reads the passage and draws curved lines under each phrase.

- Have your students do a lot of reading – at a level they can read independently. The more we practice, the better at something we get. Make sure readers are reading at their independent reading level, and give them at least 20 minutes each school day to read on their own.

## Sight Words:

| | | | | | |
|---|---|---|---|---|---|
| all | did | must | ride | too | with |
| am | do | new | saw | under | yes |
| are | eat | no | say | want | |
| at | four | now | she | was | |
| ate | get | on | so | well | |
| be | good | our | soon | went | |
| black | have | out | that | what | |
| brown | he | please | there | white | |
| but | into | pretty | they | who | |
| came | like | ran | this | will | |

# Focus on Fluency

## Strong readers focus on fluency!

| Expression | pay attention to the characters' feelings and show it in your voice. |
|---|---|
| Rate | Do not read too fast or too slow. Read like you talk. |
| Phrasing | Read in smooth phrases. (Readers who read one word at a time usually sound choppy. |
| Punctuation | Pay attention to punctuation! (Stop at a period. Pause at a comma.) |
| Accuracy | Think about what you are reading. If it doesn't make sense, go back and reread it. |
| Intonation | Make your voice go up, go down, become louder, or become softer. |
| Stress | Read words in italics with more force. Emphasize certain words. |
| | Self-assessment |

1. Accuracy - Did what you read made sense?
2. Rate - Did you read too fast, too slow, or just the right speed?
3. Phrasing - Did you read in smooth phrases or in choppy chunks?
4. Punctuation - Did you pay attention to punctuation?
5. Expression - Did you show the characters' feelings in your voice?
6. Intonation - Did your voice go up and down? Did your voice get louder and softer?
7. Stress - Did you emphasize words in italics?

# Fluency Rubric

|   | Expression and Volume |
|---|---|
| 1 | Reads in a quiet voice as if to get words out. The reading does not sound natural like talking to a friend. |
| 2 | Reads in a quiet voice. The reading sounds natural in part of the text, but the reader does not always sound like they are talking to a friend. |
| 3 | Reads with volume and expression. However, sometimes the reader slips into expressionless reading and does not sound like they are talking to a friend. |
| 4 | Reads with varied volume and expression. The reader sounds like they are talking to a friend with their voice matching the interpretation of the passage. |
|   | **Phrasing** |
| 1 | Reads word-by-word in a monotone voice. |
| 2 | Reads in two or three word phrases, not adhering to punctuation, stress and intonation. |
| 3 | Reads with a mixture of run-ons, mid sentence pauses for breath, and some choppiness. There is reasonable stress and intonation. |
| 4 | Reads with good phrasing; adhering to punctuation, stress and intonation. |
|   | **Smoothness** |
| 1 | Frequently hesitates while reading, sounds out words, and repeats words or phrases. The reader makes multiple attempts to read the same passage. |
| 2 | Reads with extended pauses or hesitations. The reader has many "rough spots." |

| | |
|---|---|
| 3 | Reads with occasional breaks in rhythm. The reader has difficulty with specific words and/or sentence structures. |
| 4 | Reads smoothly with some breaks, but self-corrects with difficult words and/ or sentence structures. |
| | |
| | **Pace** |
| 1 | Reads slowly and laboriously. |
| 2 | Reads moderately slow. |
| 3 | Reads fast and slow throughout reading. |
| 4 | Reads at a conversational pace throughout the reading. |
| | Score _____ <br><br>Scores of 10 or more indicate that the student is making good progress in fluency.<br><br>Scores below 10 indicate that the student needs additional instruction in fluency. |

| | **Reading Fluency Rating Scale** |
|---|---|
| 1 | Reading is clearly labored, very slow pace, disfluent reading. |
| 2 | Reading is somewhat slow pace and choppy. |
| 3 | Poor phrasing and intonation, but with reasonable pace. |
| | |
| | |
| | |

# Reading Comprehension

## Understanding what I read!

**Three ways to read a book:**
1. Read the pictures.
2. Read the words.
3. Re-read the story.

**Reading Strategies**
1. Look at the picture.
2. Say the beginning sound.
3. Slowly stretch each letter sound to make the word. ship = sh iii p
4. Try to re-read the sentence.
5. Break the word into chunks you already know. m at, fl at, splatter.
6. Flip the vowel sound. Try the long and short sounds.
7. Skip the tricky word. Read to the end. Go back and try it again.

Question words that make me think. Can you answer questions about a story you read?

| Who? | What? | Where? |
|---|---|---|
| A person or animal. | An object or action. | A place. |
| Who will be at school? | What is that?  That is my birthday gift. | Where do you live? |

| When? | Why? | How? |
|---|---|---|
| A time. | A reason or explanation. | A number (how many, often, much) or a way things are done. |
| When do you go to sleep?<br><br>Momo goes to bed at 8:30 p.m. | Why can't I use the scissors? | How many times have you been to Kakata?<br><br>How do you go to Kakata? |

## Simple Sentences

I like yam.
Who are you?
The fan is on.
Can I sit by you?
We all love to read.
I like to write stories.
He is going to school.

What is your name?
This gift is for Zaq.
There are two birds in the tree.
I ate a banana and an orange.

## First and Then

First your socks, **then** your shoes.
First one, **then** two.
First hide, **then** seek.
You find me, **then** I will find you.

Pratice reading workbook pages 110 to 129.

Practical

## Sam Likes Yam

Sam is my brother.
He likes ham and yam.
Mama gave Sam some ham.
Does he like jam?
No, Sam likes ham and yam.

1. Sam likes _____
    a. Yam
    b. Egg
    c. Gum
2. Sam likes _____
    a. jam
    b. ham
    c. Gum
3. Does Sam like jam?
    a. yes
    b. no

## Three Little Flies

I see a jar.
The jar has a lid.
The flies are in the jar.
I see three flies.

1. I see a _____.
    a. pan
    b. jar
    c. mat
2. The _____ are in the jar.
    a. bugs
    b. frogs
    c. flies
3. I see _____ in the jar.
    a. two
    b. three
    c. four

## Musu's Pink Bike

Musu loves her new bike.
She rides it in the church yard.
Musu's bike is pink.
She got her bike for her birthday.

Who has a bike?
What color is it? Where did Musu get her bike?

## A Visit to the Zoo

Zaq went to the zoo. He saw a big elephant eating peanuts.
Zaq saw a lion at the zoo. It was big and scary.
The giraffe was very tall. It likes to eat leaves.
The monkey was silly. It likes to play in the tree.
Zaq had fun at the zoo.

Who went to the zoo?
What was big and scary?
Where did the monkey like to play?
Did Zaq have fun?

## My Cat Yoyo

My cat Yoyo likes to play!
He likes to jump and chase rats.
Yoyo also likes to play with a red ball.
Best of all, Yoyo likes to watch the chicks follow their mother hen.

1. What is the cat's name?
2. What does Yoyo like to chase?
3. What color ball does Yoyo like to play with?
4. What does Yoyo like best of all?

## On the Farm

We are going to take pictures of animals.
I see a hen!
Let's take a picture.
Look! I see four chicks!
There are two big goats and one little kid.
We also saw a rooster, two pigs, and a great big cow!

1. What do Ian and Little Bea want to do at the farm?
2. How many pigs did they see?
3. What kind of animals did they take pictures of?
4. What other kinds of animals live on the farm?

## What is Wrong with Blaze?

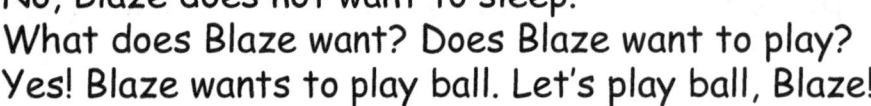

Blaze is sad. Why is Blaze sad?
Does Blaze want a bone?
No, Blaze does not want a bone.
What is wrong with Blaze?
Why is Blaze sad?
Does Blaze want to sleep?
No, Blaze does not want to sleep.
What does Blaze want? Does Blaze want to play?
Yes! Blaze wants to play ball. Let's play ball, Blaze!

1. What is wrong with Blaze?
2. How does Blaze feel?
3. Does Blaze want to sleep?
4. Why do you think Blaze wants to play ball?
5. If you had a dog, what would you do to make sure your dog is happy?

## Bugs!

We like bugs!
We like to look at bugs in a jar.
Momo put three bugs in his jar.
Hawa likes to look at bugs, too!
Hawa is happy because she found 2 lightning bugs.
When we are done looking at the bugs, we like to let them go!

1. Why do the kids like to collect bugs?
2. Why was Hawa happy?
3. What do the kids do with the bugs after they look at them?
4. Do you have a favorite kind of bug?

## Nanny's Surprise

Nanny has a surprise.
What could it be?
Is it hay? No, it is not hay.
What is Nanny's surprise?
Is it a new brush?
No, it is not a new brush.
I know Nanny's surprise!
Nanny had a baby kid!
"Mehh," said the baby kid!

1. What does Nanny have?
2. Where do you think the story takes place?
3. What are the two things that were not Nanny's surprise?
4. How do you think Nanny feels?

## We-Care Library

Flomo likes to read folktale books.
Flomo has read 5 books about Spider and Elephant.
He wants to read more.
Korlu likes to read books about dolls.
Korlu wishes she could have a doll.
Going to We-Care Library is fun!
You can read many books at the We-Care Library.
You can read about many new things.

1. What kind of books does Flomo like to read?
2. What types of books does Korlu like to read?
3. What can you do at the library?
4. What kind of books do you like to read?

## Korlu's Birthday

I have a balloon for Korlu's birthday.
I can give Korlu a balloon.
Korlu will like a balloon.
I have a present for Korlu.
Korlu will like my present.
I have a toy for Korlu.
I have a dog for Korlu!
Do you think Korlu will like a dog?

1. Who is the main character in the story?
2. What does the first boy give Korlu for her birthday?
3. What kind of present did the girl give to Korlu for her birthday?
4. What would you give Korlu for her birthday?

## I am a Bookworm

I am a bookworm because I like to read.
My favorite place to read is at my desk.
We have many books in my class library.
We have 42 books in my class library!
I am a bookworm and I love to read!
Are you a bookworm, too?

1. What is a bookworm?
2. Where is the girl's favorite place to read?
3. Why do you think the girl has so many books?
4. Do you think you are a bookworm, too?

# The Doctor's Bag

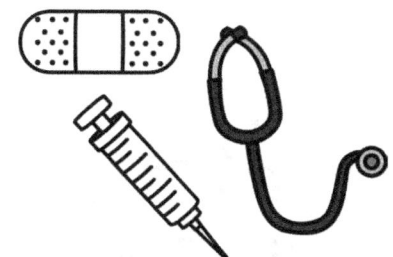
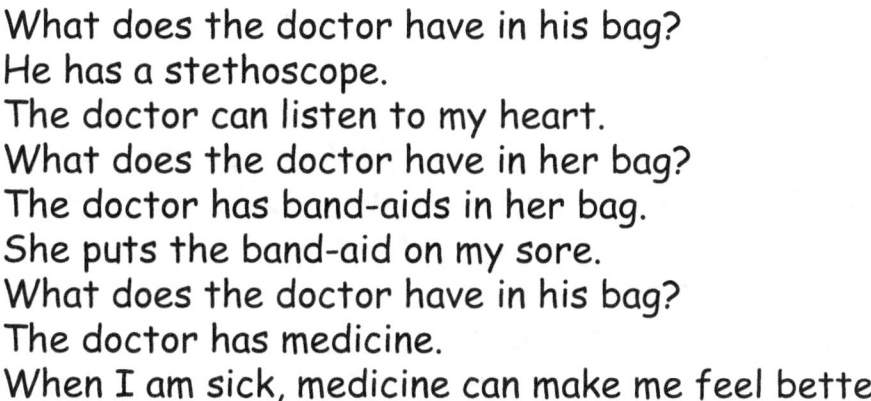

What does the doctor have in his bag?
He has a stethoscope.
The doctor can listen to my heart.
What does the doctor have in her bag?
The doctor has band-aids in her bag.
She puts the band-aid on my sore.
What does the doctor have in his bag?
The doctor has medicine.
When I am sick, medicine can make me feel better.

1. Who is the main character in the story?
2. What does a doctor do with a stethoscope?
3. Why does the doctor give you medicine?
4. What else might a doctor have in their bag?

# Pawpaw Pie

I want to make a pawpaw pie.
I need green pawpaws to make my pawpaw pie.
What kind of pawpaws should I use?
I have three small pawpaws.
I have two big yellow pawpaws.
I have four green pawpaws.
Which pawpaws should I use?
I will use all of the green pawpaws to make a delicious pawpaw pie.
I will drink ginger juice with my pawpaw pie! Yum!

1. What does the boy want to make?
2. What kind of pawpaws does he have?
3. How many pawpaws did he use to make a pawpaw pie?
4. What else might you need to make a pawpaw pie?

# Laundry

Mama likes to wash clothes three days a week.
On Monday she washes the white clothes.
Mama washes the dark clothes on Wednesday.
On Friday, Mama washes the towels and hang them out to dry.

1. Who is the main character in the story?
2. What does Mama do on Monday?
3. What does Mama do on Wednesday?
4. Why does Mama hang the towels?

# Football

Momo likes to play football.
He is really good at getting the ball into the goal.
Hawa likes to play football, too!
Hawa is really good at dribbling the ball!
Ballah likes to play football.
Ballah is really good at passing the ball.

1. What is Momo really good at?
2. Does Hawa like to play football? What is Hawa good at?
3. What does Ballah do well?
4. What are you really good at?

# Bubble Gum

Hawa likes bubble gum!
Hawa can blow a small bubble.
Momo likes bubble gum, too.
Momo can blow a medium-sized bubble.
Fatu loves bubble gum!
Fatu can blow a very big bubble!

1. What is the story about?
2. Who blew a medium-sized bubble?
3. Who blew the biggest bubble?
4. How do you blow a bubble?

# Read and Sequence

## FLUENCY and COMPREHENSION through SEQUENCING STORY EVENTS

Direction: Read the story, number the pictures according to the order of events.
1. What happens FIRST?
2. What happened NEXT?
3. THEN what happened?
4. What happened LAST?

| Let's Put it in the Bag | | | |
|---|---|---|---|
| What can we put in the brown bag? Can I put a hat in the bag? Yes, put it in. Can I put my ball in the bag? Yes. You can put the purple sock in the bag. Do not put the dirty pig in the bag! ||||
| **1** FIRST, | **2** NEXT, | **3** THEN, | **4** LAST |
| | | | |

98

## What is on the T-shirt

Little Gola has a lot of t-shirts.
Gola has a rabbit on her t-shirt.
She likes the t-shirt with the big elephant.
She has a t-shirt with a small rat.
Gola likes the monkey on her t-shirt.

| 1 FIRST, | 2 NEXT, | 3 THEN, | 4 LAST |
|---|---|---|---|
| | | | |

## Who Can Go in the House?

Can a snake go in the house? No, not a snake.
Do you see chickens in the house? No, not chickens.
Do pigs go in a house? No, no pigs in the house.
Can I go in the house? Yes! I can go in the house.

| 1 FIRST, | 2 NEXT, | 3 THEN, | 4 LAST |
|---|---|---|---|
| | | | |

Read the story below. Highlight all the sequence words you see in the story. Number the story according to the order of events.

### Where is the Cricket?

The cricket hid. Where did he go?
The cricket is on my bed! Go away, cricket!
Oh no! the cricket is on the mat! Go away, cricket!
The cricket is on Mama's hat! No, no cricket!
I see the cricket in the mud. That is O.K.

| 1 FIRST, | 2 NEXT, | 3 THEN, | 4 LAST |
|---|---|---|---|
| | | | |
| | | | |

### Peanut Butter and Jelly Sandwich

Every day Fatu makes her favorite snack to eat for lunch. First, Fatu takes all the ingredients out of the cupboard. Next, she gets two slices of bread and set them on a plate. Then, she spreads peanut butter and jelly onto the bread and put them together. Finally, Fatu sits down and eat her delicious PB&J sandwich.

| 1 FIRST, | 2 NEXT, | 3 THEN, | 4 LAST |
|---|---|---|---|

#### What did Fatu do first?

Number the story according to the order of events.

| Fatu eats her PB&J sandwich. | Fatu gets two slices of bread. | Fatu puts peanut butter and jelly on the bread. | Fatu gets all the ingredients. |
|---|---|---|---|
| | | | |

# Washing Your Hands

Read the story below. Highlight all the sequence words you see in the story. Number the story according to the order of events.

First, turn on the water and make sure it is warm water. Next, squirt a dab of soap onto the palm of your hands. Rub your hands together for 1 minute. Then rinse your hands with water. Last, dry your hands with a towel.

What happens after you rinse your hands?

| | | Rinse your hands with water. |
|---|---|---|
| | | Turn on warm water. |
| | | Dry your hands with a towel. |
| | | Squirt soap into your hand. |
| **1** FIRST, | **2** NEXT, | **3** THEN, | **4** LAST |

Read the story below. Write all the sequence words missing in the story. Number the story according to the order of events.

| | | Pawpaw Pie |
|---|---|---|
| | | Mama and I went to the market. |
| | | We went home. |
| | | We picked out three green pawpaws. |
| | | Mama made a pie with the pawpaws. |
| | | We put the pawpaws in the basket. |
| | | Mama paid for the pawpaws. |

# Guided Reading Lesson Plan

This system gives data and proof of what the teacher has been working on, and shows the growth of individual students.

Prepare your lesson plan, determine the skill(s) to be worked on, the book which will be used. Choose activities to do before, during and after the reading.

List individual students and add skill, goals, notes taken while the student is reading, and the feedback to give to the student.

| Guided Reading Lesson | | | |
|---|---|---|---|
| Word Work | | Vocabulary | |
| 1. 2. 3. 4. 5. | 6. 7. 8. 9. 10 | 1. 2. 3. 4. 5. | 6. 7. 8. 9. 10 |
| **Before Reading** | | | |
| [] Predict<br>[] Picture Walk<br>[] Access prior knowldge<br>[] Questions | | [] KWL Chart<br>[] Difficult Vocabulary<br>[] Personal Connection<br>[] Text Features | [] Author's Purpose<br>[] Skim the Text |
| **During Reading** | | | |
| [] Think Aloud<br>[] Turn & Talk<br>[] I Notice . . .<br>[] Comprehension Questions | | [] Text Features<br>[] Point out Vocabulary<br>[] Personal Connection<br>[] Context Clues | [] Check Predictions |
| **After Reading** | | | |
| [] Retell (BME}<br>[] Summarize<br>[] Compare to another book<br>[] Repeated Reading | | [] Text Features<br>[] Point out Vocabulary<br>[] Personal Connections<br>[] Context Clues | [] Questions |

# Primary Arithmetic

Process Skills
- Use appropriate technology to solve mathematical problems.
- Build new mathematical knowledge through problem-solving.
- Solve problems that arise in mathematics and in other areas.
- Apply and adapt a variety of appropriate strategies to solve problems.
- Monitor and reflect on the process of mathematical problem-solving
- Recognize reasoning and proof (evidence) as fundamental aspects of mathematics.
- Make and investigate mathematical conjectures.
- Investigate, develop, and evaluate mathematical arguments and proofs.
- Select and use various types of reasoning and methods of proof.
- Organize and consolidate mathematics thinking.
- Communicate mathematical thinking coherently to peers, teachers, and others.
- Analyze and evaluate the mathematical thinking and strategies of others.
- Use the terminology and language of mathematics to express mathematical ideas precisely.
- Recognize and use connections among mathematical ideas.
- Explain how mathematical ideas interconnect and build on one another to produce a coherent whole.
- Recognize and apply mathematics in contexts outside of mathematics
- Create and use pictures, manipulative, models, and symbols to organize, record, and communicate mathematical ideas.
- Select, apply, and translate among mathematical representations to solve problems.
- Use representations to model and interpret physical, social, and mathematical phenomena.

Numbers and Operations
- Demonstrate one-to-one correspondence when counting objects through 30.
- Produce models for number words through 10.
- Match numerals to sets through 20.
- Recognize and write numerals through 20 to label sets.
- Sequence and identify ordinal numbers 1st through 10th.
- Compare two or more sets of objects (1-10) and identify which set is equal to, more than, or less than the other.
- Estimate quantities using five and 10 as benchmarks (e.g., 9 is one five and four more which is closer to two fives or one 10 than it is to one five)
- Use informal strategies to share objects equally between two or three people or sets.
- Identify Liberian dollars by name and value: 5, 10, 20, 50, 100 Liberian dollars.
- Count out Liberian dollars to buy items that together cost less than 50 Liberian dollars.
- Make fair trades involving combinations of 5, 10, 20 Liberian dollars.
- Use counting strategies to find out how many items are in two sets when they are combined, separated, or compared.
- Build number combinations up to 10.
- Use objects, pictures, numbers, or words to create, solve, and explain story problems for two numbers that are each less than 10 (including the concepts of joining, separating, or comparing objects)

Geometry
- Recognize, name, and sort geometric figures: triangles, rectangles, squares, circles.
- Compare geometric shapes and identify similarities and differences of the following two and three-dimensional figures: triangles, rectangles, squares, circles, spheres, and cubes.
- Recognize and name spheres and cubes.
- Identify concrete objects in the environment and represent the objects using basic shapes.
- Combine basic shapes into basic and more complicated shapes.

- Decompose basic shapes into combinations of basic shapes.
- Identify spatial relationships, such as when an object is beside, above, below, in front of, behind, inside, or outside another object.

Measurement
- Compare and order objects on the basis of length(longer/shorter), capacity (more/less), height (taller/shorter), and weight (heavier/lighter) (GPS)
- Name days of the week, months of the year, and the two seasons.
- Use the words yesterday, today, and tomorrow, to describe the passage of time and to order daily events.
- Tell the time when daily events occur, such as morning, afternoon, and night.
- Name the day of the week when weekly events occur in class.

Algebra
- Identify, create, extend, and transfer patterns from one representation to another using actions, objects, and geometric shapes.
- Identify missing shapes within a given pattern of geometric shapes
- Extend a given pattern and recognize similarities, such as color, shape, texture, or number, in different patterns.
- Explore the concept of equivalence relating to addition and subtraction, such as a set represented by 4+1 is equivalent to a set represented by 3+2.
- Sort and categorize objects by identifying attributes such as longer/shorter, more/less, taller/shorter, and heavier/lighter, and make generalizations.

Data Analysis and Probability
- Pose information questions, collect and organize data, and record results using objects, pictures, and picture graphs.

# Math and Numbers

You have to know your numbers so you can learn math.
You have to know your numbers so you can count.
You have to know your numbers to know how much money you have.

## Math Shows How Numbers Work

| Math tell us how many things we have. | Zaq has 2 new toys. I have 3 cupcakes. |
|---|---|
| Math shows the size of something. | The cat is only 7 inches long. This giraffe is 10 feet tall. |
| Math lets us know how far a place is. | Monrovia is three miles away. |

 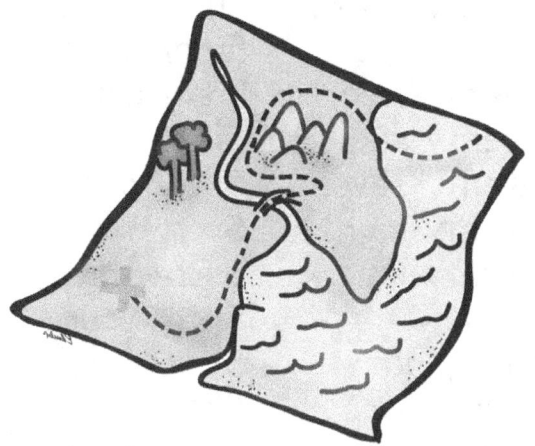

# Number Words

| | | |
|---|---|---|
| Zero | Thirty-four | Sixty-eight |
| One | Thirty-five | Sixty-nine |
| Two | Thirty-six | Seventy |
| Three | Thirty-seven | Seventy-one |
| Four | Thirty-eight | Seventy-two |
| Five | Thirty-nine | Seventy-three |
| Six | Forty | Seventy-four |
| Seven | Forty-one | Seventy-five |
| Eight | Forty-two | Seventy-six |
| Nine | Forty-three | Seventy-seven |
| Ten | Forty-four | Seventy-eight |
| Eleven | Forty-five | Seventy-nine |
| Twelve | Forty-six | Eighty |
| Thirteen | Forty-seven | Eighty-one |
| Fourteen | Forty-eight | Eighty-two |
| Fifteen | Forty-nine | Eighty-three |
| Sixteen | Fifty | Eighty-four |
| Seventeen | Fifty-one | Eighty-five |
| Eight-teen | Fifty-two | Eighty-six |
| Nineteen | Fifty-three | Eighty-seven |
| Twenty | Fifty-four | Eighty-eight |
| Twenty-one | Fifty-five | Eighty-nine |
| Twenty-two | Fifty-six | Ninety |
| Twenty-three | Fifty-seven | Ninety-one |
| Twenty-four | Fifty-eight | Ninety-two |
| Twenty-five | Fifty-nine | Ninety-three |
| Twenty-six | Sixty | Ninety-four |
| Twenty-seven | Sixty-one | Ninety-five |
| Twenty-eight | Sixty-two | Ninety-six |
| Twenty-nine | Sixty-three | Ninety-seven |
| Thirty | Sixty-four | Ninety-eight |
| Thirty-one | Sixty-five | Ninety-nine |
| Thirty-two | Sixty-six | One hundred |
| Thirty-three | Sixty-seven | |

## Addition Word List

total
altogether
join
both
sum
combined
increase
together
add
plus

5 + 1 = 6

Gus the Plus is a generous young man,
giving to others whenever he can!

He will show you how many you have in all,
when he comes around your sum will grow tall!

He adds numbers together so that you will have more,
With help from Gus adding is never a chore!

## Subtraction Word List

How many more?
decrease
less than
take away
minus
difference
left
remains
fewer
shorter
faster
longer
subtract
How much more?

5 − 1 = 4

Linus the Minus is a naughty rabbit,
always taking away.
He is oh so bad!

When he comes around you will end up with less!
He makes a big difference,
but he will never confess!

# Addition Strategies

Use your fingers to add numbers.
Color the fingers to show the equation:
**3+4=7**

Use snap cubes to add numbers.
Use 2 colors to show the equation: **4+6=10**

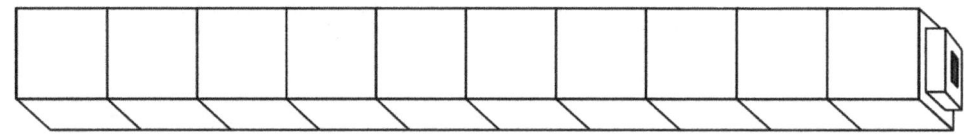

Use a number line to add numbers.
Use the number line to show the equation:
**5+5=10**

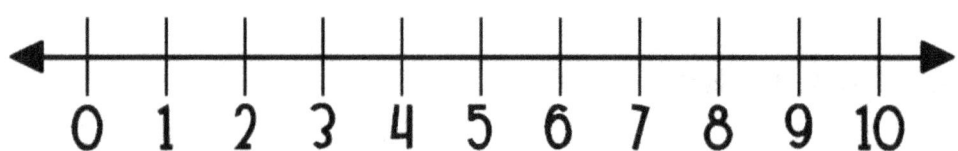

Use ten frames to add numbers.
Use the ten frame to show the equation:
**7+3=10**

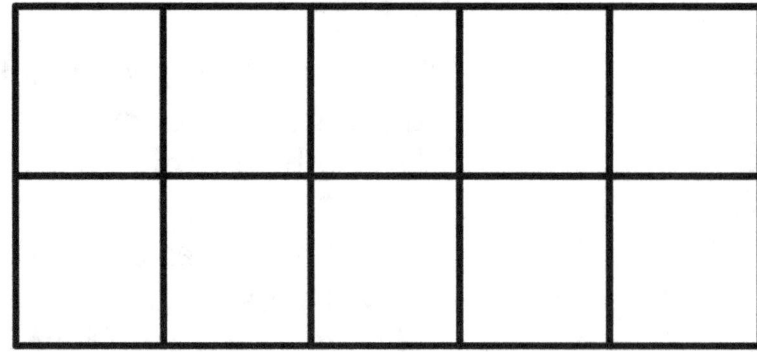

## Counters

Using counters to add numbers; like rocks, marbles, or sticks. Draw pictures of your counters to show the equation: **1+9=10**

## Count the Dots and Write the number below.

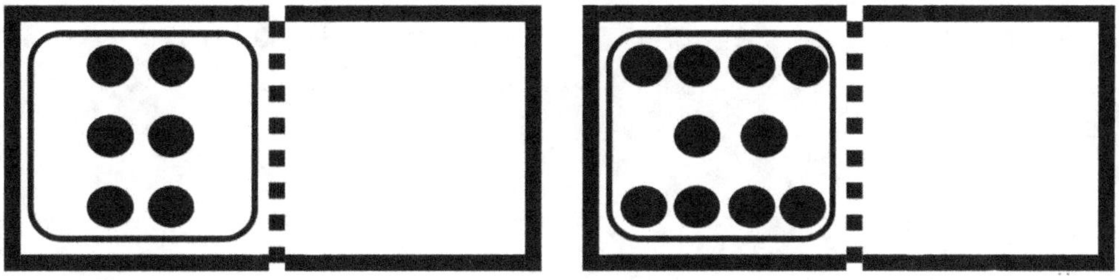

Draw pictures of dots to show the equation: 1+9=10

## Addition

1 + 1 = 2

3 + 1 = 4

4 + 1 = 5

0 + 1 = 1

3 + 1 = 4

2 + 1 = 3

# Domino Addition

Count the number of dots on each domino and write the numbers on the lines. Add up the dots and put the sum in the box.

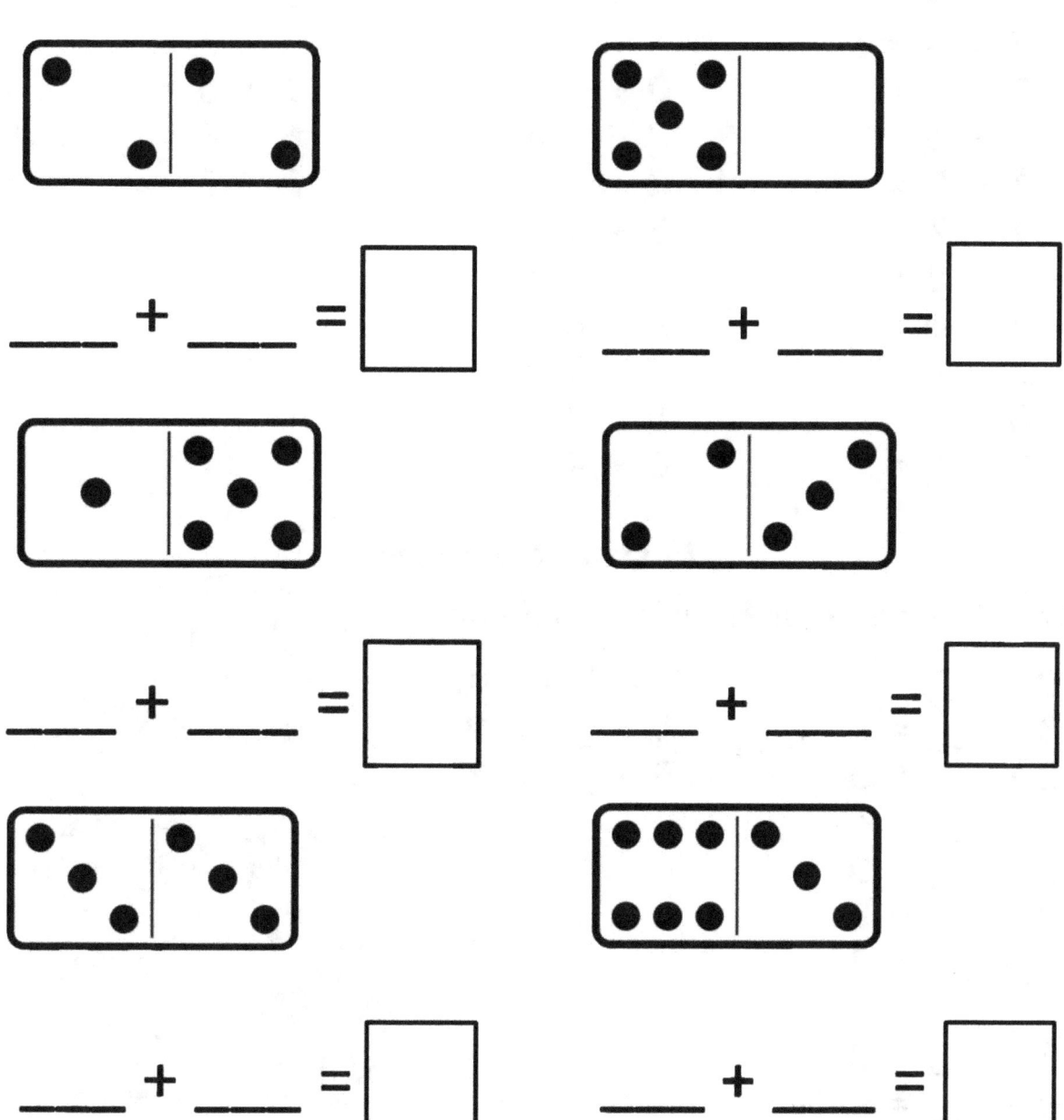

## Solve the Problems

| | | |
|---|---|---|
| 1 + 1 = | 3 + 5 = | 8 + 2 = |
| 1 + 2 = | 4 + 1 = | 5 + 5 = |
| 1 + 3 = | 5 + 1 = | 6 + 3 = |
| 2 + 2 = | 6 + 2 = | 0 + 8 = |
| 1 + 4 = | 7 + 3 = | 1 + 8 = |
| 2 + 3 = | 1 + 7 = | 0 + 7 = |
| 2 + 4 = | 0 + 3 = | 1 + 5 = |
| 2 + 5 = | 2 + 4 = | 6 + 6 = |
| 1 + 5 = | 2 + 0 = | 2 + 7 = |
| 1 + 7 = | 3 + 1 = | |
| 1 + 8 = | 3 + 7 = | |
| 1 + 6 = | 9 + 2 = | |
| 3 + 2 = | 4 + 5 = | |
| 3 + 3 = | 5 + 3 = | |
| 3 + 4 = | 6 + 4 = | |

## Missing Numbers

Write the missing number in each problem.

0 + ___ = 1        4 + ___ = 10
3 + ___ = 7        1 + ___ = 9
2 + ___ = 5        5 + ___ = 7
3 + ___ = 4
1 + ___ = 5
2 + ___ = 2
1 + ___ = 3
0 + ___ = 4
2 + ___ = 3
4 + ___ = 5
2 + ___ = 6

# Tell the Truth

Solve the equations to tell if they are true or false.

| 0 + 5 = 5 | 2 + 2 = 4 | 3 + 1 = 2 |
|---|---|---|
| True  False | True  False | True  False |
| ☐    ☐ | ☐    ☐ | ☐    ☐ |

| 1 + 1 = 2 | 2 + 1 = 4 | 1 + 4 = 5 |
|---|---|---|
| True  False | True  False | True  False |
| ☐    ☐ | ☐    ☐ | ☐    ☐ |

| 3 + 3 = 6 | 2 + 5 = 7 | 0 + 1 = 0 |
|---|---|---|
| True  False | True  False | True  False |
| ☐    ☐ | ☐    ☐ | ☐    ☐ |

| 6 + 1 = 5 | 4 + 1 = 3 | 8 + 1 = 9 |
|---|---|---|
| True  False | True  False | True  False |
| ☐    ☐ | ☐    ☐ | ☐    ☐ |

# Fishing for Equations

Use the numbers inside each fish to write 3 addition equations.

___ + ___ = ___

___ + ___ = ___

___ + ___ = ___

___ + ___ = ___

___ + ___ = ___

___ + ___ = ___

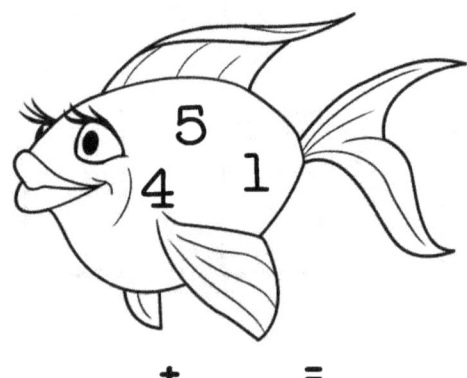

___ + ___ = ___

___ + ___ = ___

___ + ___ = ___

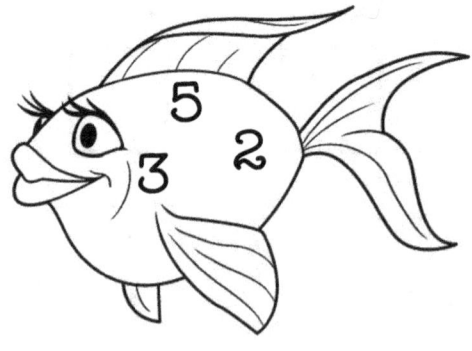

___ + ___ = ___

___ + ___ = ___

___ + ___ = ___

# Seeing Double

Write each sum to its doubles' fact.

  2
___ + ___ = ___

  4
___ + ___ = ___

  6
___ + ___ = ___

  10
___ + ___ = ___

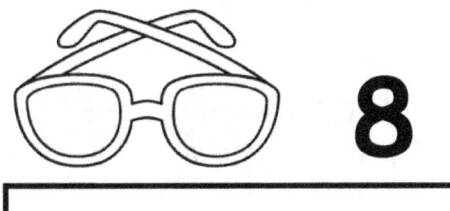  8
___ + ___ = ___

1 + 1

2 + 2

3 + 3

4 + 4

5 + 5

## Subtraction Action

**Take Away -**
How many more? How much more?
Cross out objects to show subtraction.

**Cross out objects to show subtraction.**

4 - 1 = ___

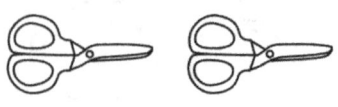

2 - 2 = ___

 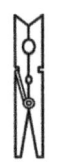 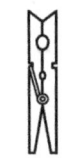 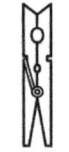 

5 - 4 = ___

3 - 1 = ___

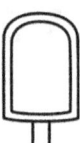   

4 - 4 = ___

 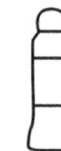 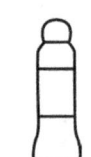

3 - 0 = ___

3 - 2 = ___

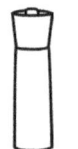  

3 - 3 = ___

 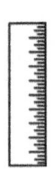   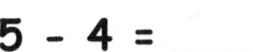

5 - 2 = ___

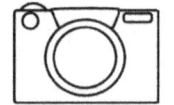 

2 - 0 = ___

# Subtraction Facts

Count the fingers and use them to help you solve the problems.

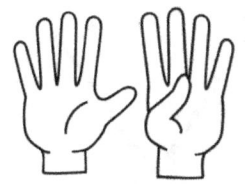 -  = ____     8 - 3 =

5 - 4 =

8 - 8 =

 -  = ____     9 - 5 =

4 - 2 =

10 - 7 =

 -  = ____

 -  = ____     **ten 10**

10 - 1 =

 -  = ____     10 - 4 =

10 - 6 =

10 - 8 =

 -  = ____     10 - 10 =

119

# Shapes

The corners of the shapes are called, "vertices".

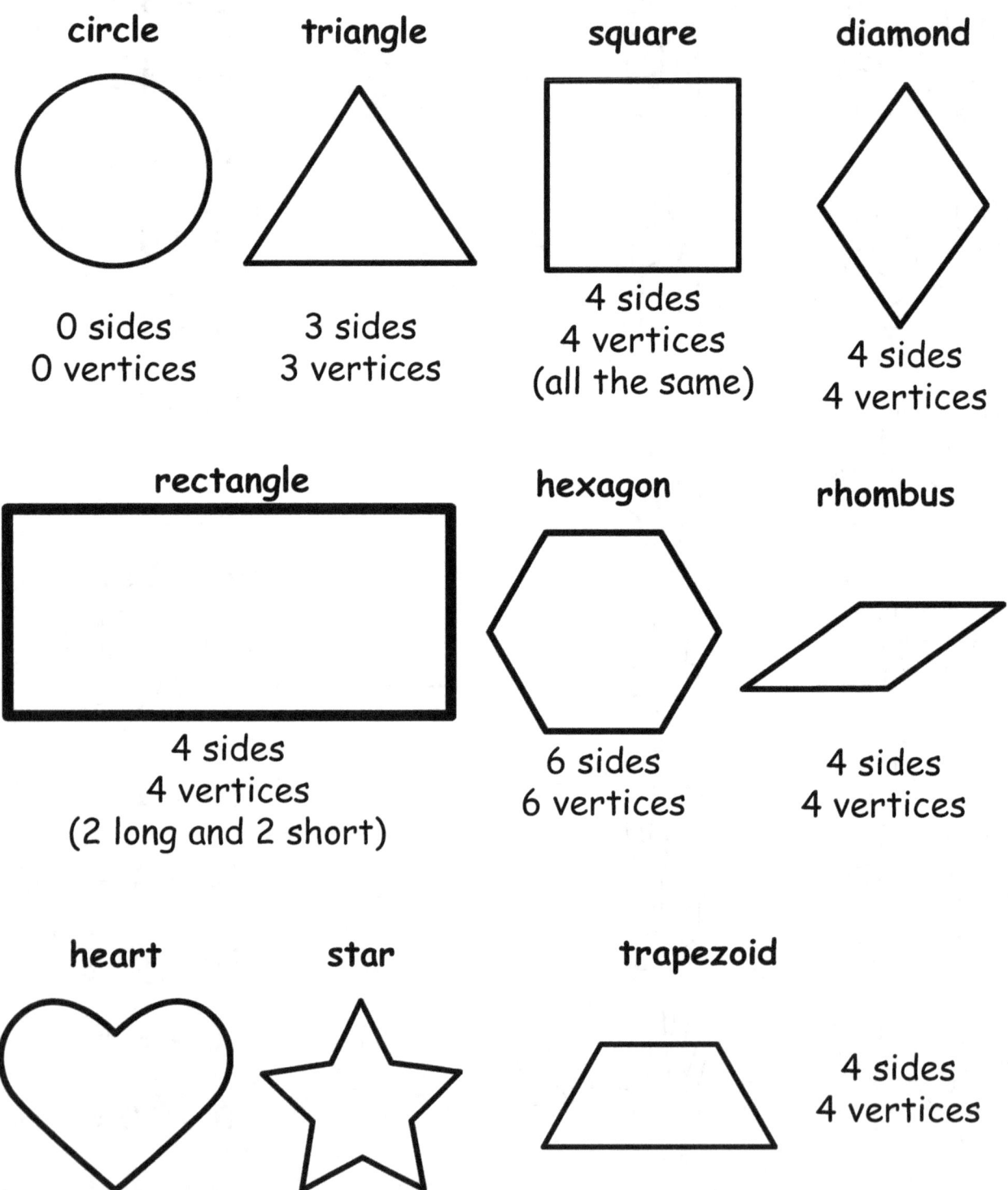

**oval**

0 sides
0 vertices

**sphere**

Looks like a ball.

**pyramid**

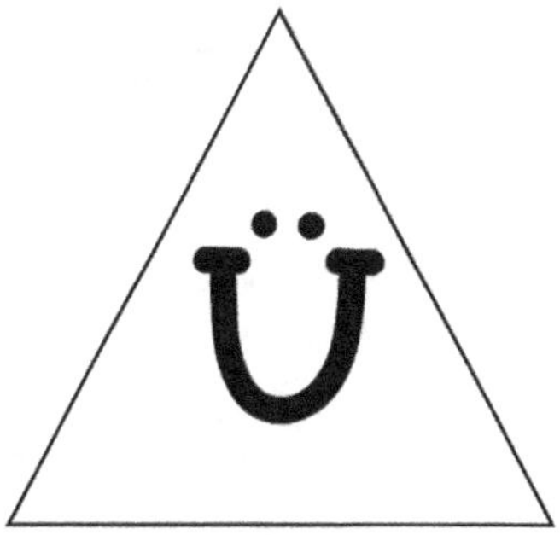

Looks like a pyramid of Egypt.

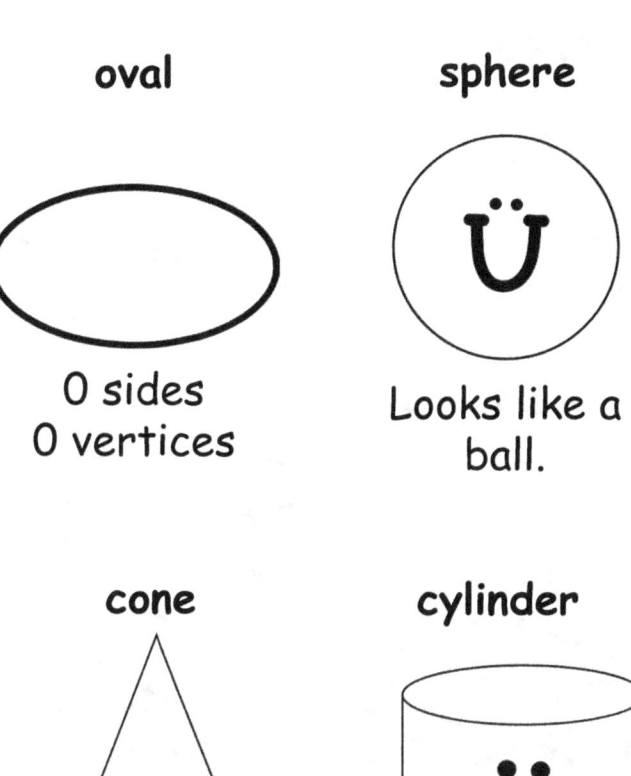

**cone**

Looks like a party hat.

**cylinder**

Looks like a can.

**cube**

Looks like a box.

**2D Shapes**

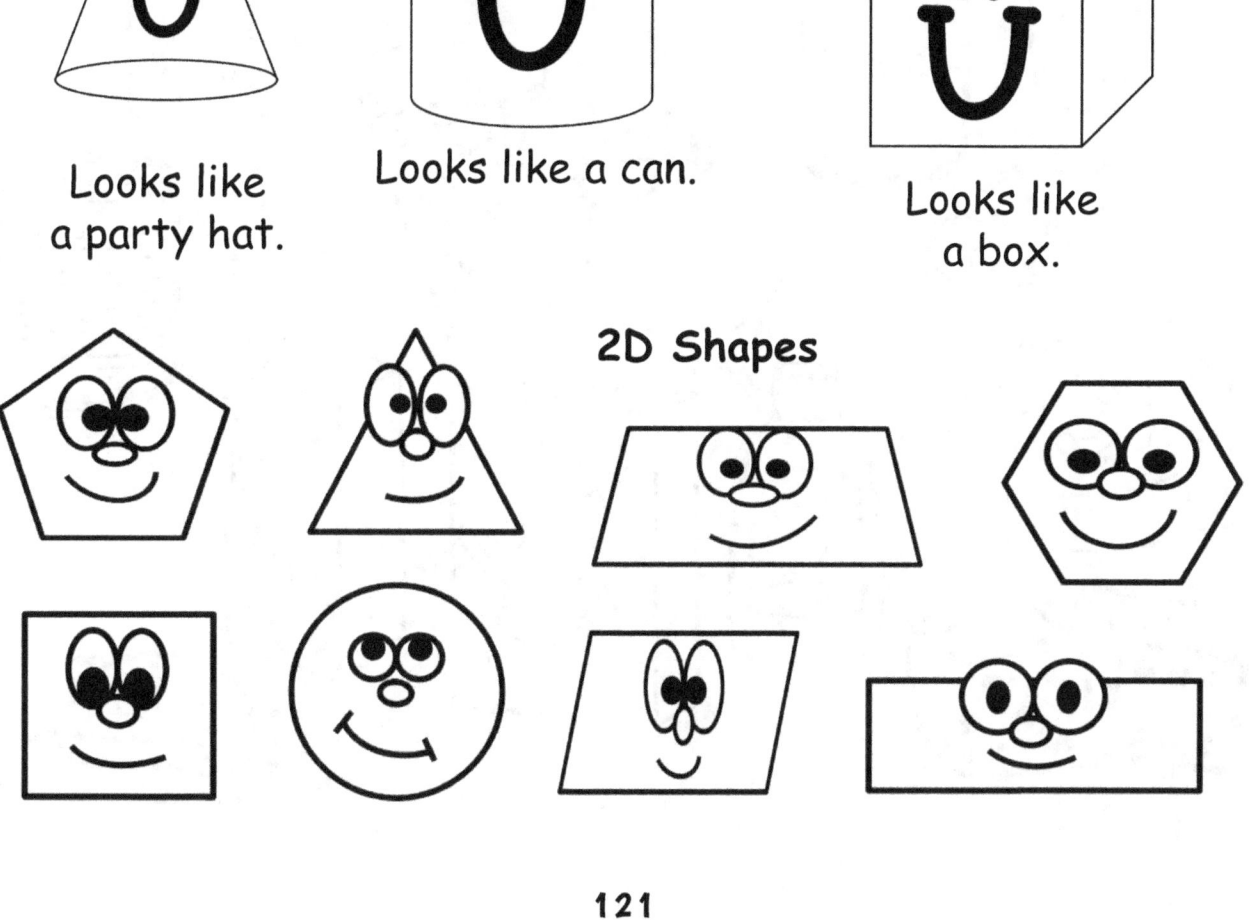

## 3D Shapes

## Everyday 3D Shapes

# Order
To put into a particular way. What comes first; what comes next!

## Number Order

| | |
|---|---|
| 1 | 6 |
| 2 | 7 |
| 3 | 8 |
| 4 | 9 |
| 5 | 10 |

## Ordinal Numbers
### Place of position order

| | |
|---|---|
| 1st first | 6th sixth |
| 2nd second | 7th seventh |
| 3rd third | 8th eighth |
| 4th fouth | 9th nineth |
| 5th fifth | 10th tenth |

## Passage of Time Order

yesterday | today | tomorrow

**Daily events occur**

morning

afternoon

night

## Weekdays in order.

Sunday
Monday
Tuesday
Wednesday
Thursday
Friday
Saturday

## Months in order.

January
February
March
April
May
June
July
August
September
October
November
December

# Left and Right Position

## Which is left and which is right?

Circle the left fly

Circle the right chips

# Place Preposition

in          on          under

between

# Occupying Space

Musu is **above** the tag.

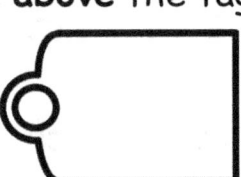

Zaq is **below** the tag.

in          out

Zaq is **outside** the box.

Musu is **inside** the box.

Musu is **behind**.          Musu is **in front**.          Musu is **beside** Zaq.

# Measuring Up!

**Capacity** - We can measure capacity. When we measure the capacity of a container, we find out how much it can hold.

**more**
The pot can hold more than the glass. It has a greater capacity.

**less**
The glass holds less than the pot. Its capacity is less.

**Weight** - When we measure the weight of something, we find out how heavy it is.

The elephant is **heavier** than the frog.
The frog is **lighter** than the elephant.

**Height** - When we measure the height of something, we find out how far it is from the bottom to the top. We find out how tall the object is.

The giraffe is **taller** than the boy.
The boy is **shorter** than the giraffe.

**Width** - When we measure the width of something, we find out how far it is from one side to the other. We find out how wide it is.

The book is **wider** than the pen.   The pen is **narrower** than the book.

**Length** - When we measure the length of something, we find out how far it is from one end to the other end. We find out how **long** the object is.

The school bus is **longer** than the car.

The car is **shorter** than the school bus.

The ruler is **longer** than the pencil.

The pencil is **shorter** than the ruler.

## Think & Talk

How fast can you think of an answer?

1. Think of three things that are **taller** than a car.
2. Think of three things that are **heavier** than a crayon.
3. Think of three things that are **wider** than a doorway.
4. Think of three things that are **lighter** than a shoe.
5. Think of three things that are **longer** than your arm.

## Comparing Objects Size

### Biggest & Smallest

### Wider & Narrower
 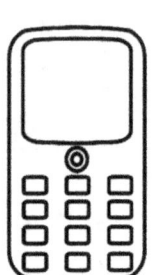

### Biger & Smaller

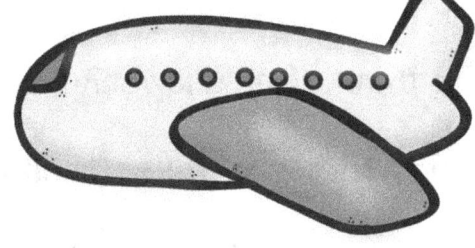

### Less & More

### Lighter & Heavier

### Shortest & Tallest

# Problem Solving

Answer the question, then tell why.

Mama is having a big party. She is going to cook jollof rice. Which pot should she use?

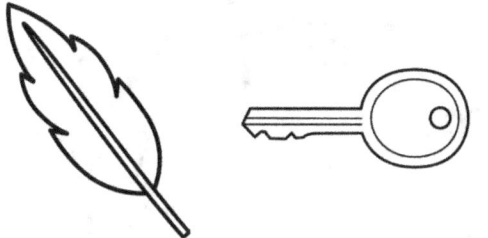
What should I tie to the end of my balloon string to keep it from floating away: a feather or a key?

If a pig and a frog were on the seesaw, whose side would touch the ground?

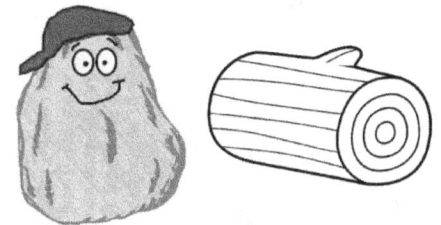
Musu needs to make a bridge to cross a stream. Should she use a log or a rock?

When packing a bag, which should you put in the bottom of the basket: eggs or pineapple?

# All About Time

60 seconds = 1 minute
60 minutes = 1 hour
24 hours = 1 day
7 days = 1 week
52 weeks = 1 year
365 days = 1 year
Decade = 10 years
Century = 100 years

We measure time using a clock.

Analog Clock

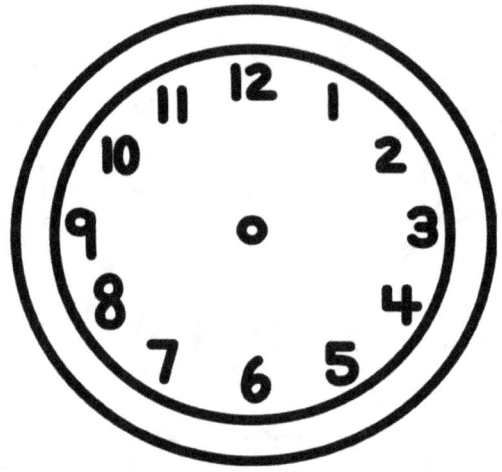

The short hand is the hour hand.

The long hand is the minute hand.

30 minutes = a half hour
The minute hand is at 6 when it is half an hour.

Digital Clock

On a digital clock, o'clock = :00

Half past the hour is :30

# Telling Time

I'm a smaller hour hand, short and stout,
I tell the hour and give a shout.
I'm a longer minute hand, big and tall,
I tell the minute and that's all.

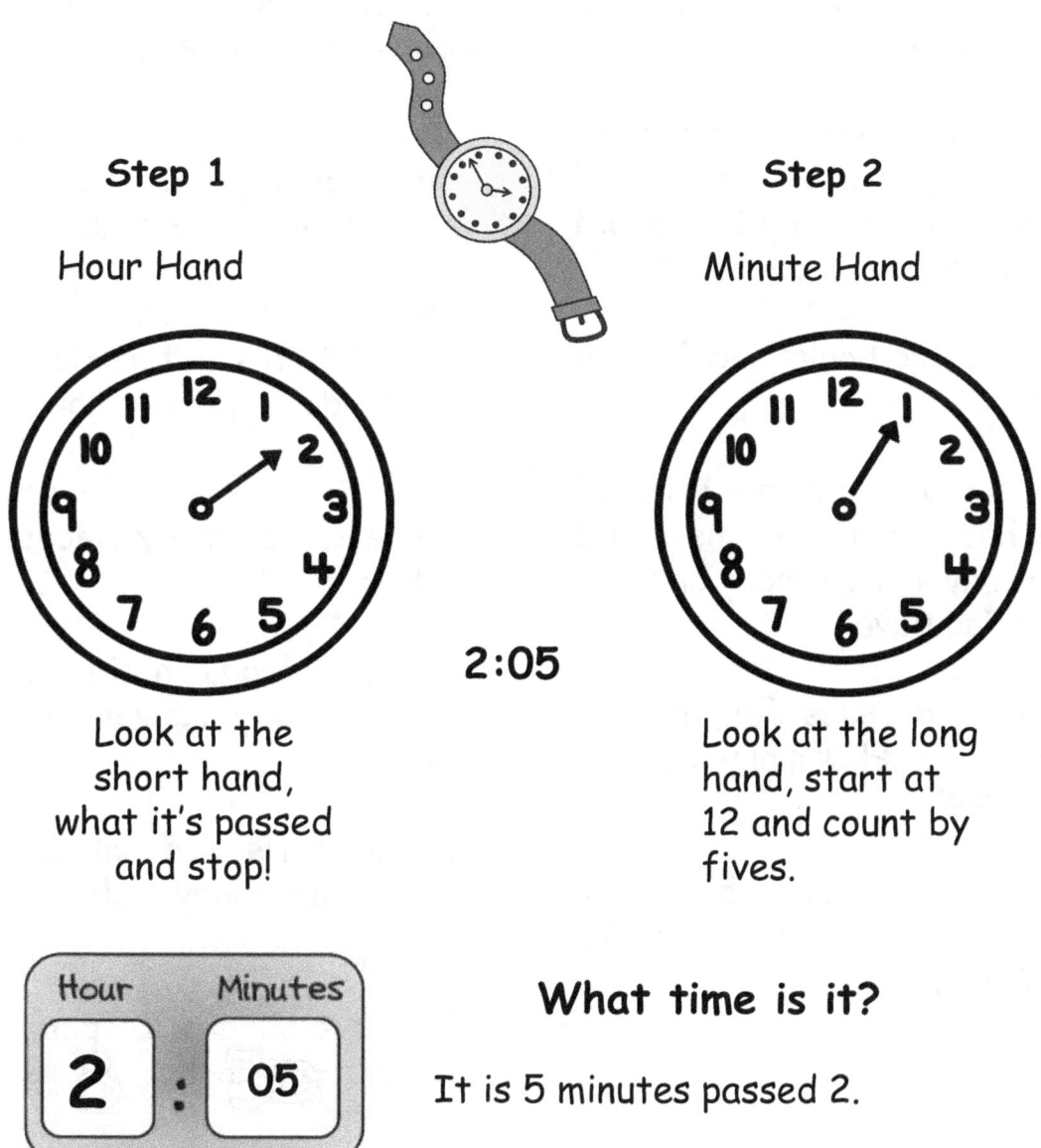

**Step 1**

Hour Hand

2:05

Look at the short hand, what it's passed and stop!

**Step 2**

Minute Hand

Look at the long hand, start at 12 and count by fives.

**What time is it?**

It is 5 minutes passed 2.

# Word Problems

## Addition

Sapo read 3 books on Monday and 2 books on Tuesday. How many books did Sapo read?

Korlu borrowed 1 book from the library and Musu borrowed 3 books. How many books did they borrow all together?

I have 2 big books and 2 little books.

How many books do I have? Zaq had 3 red crayons and 1 blue crayon. How many crayons does Zaq have?

I saw 4 oranges fall, then I saw 1 more. How many oranges did I see?

I saw 4 trucks drive by, then 1 more. How many trucks did I see?

## Take Away

I made 3 paper books. I gave 1 to my friend. How many paper books do I have now?

There are 5 boys sitting at the table and then 4 stood up. How many boys are sitting?

Ballah had 4 books and he gave 2 to his sister. How many books does he have now?

I had 5 pieces of milk candy. I ate 2. How many pieces do I have now?

I see 4 frogs in the yard. 2 jumped away. How many frogs are left?

I see 3 fish and all 3 swam away. How many fish do I see now?

I had 4 dollars. I spent 2 on a toy. How many dollars do I have now?

Mama bought 3 lollipops. She gave me 1 lollipop and gave Musu 1. How many lollipops does Mama have left?

# Currency & Money

**LRD (L$) & USD ($)**

We save our money at the bank. Ellen Johnson-Sirleaf was Liberia's first elected female president. She worked at the World Bank before she became president.

## Liberian Dollar by name and value

L$5

L$10

L$20

L$50

## What We Do With Our Money

Save    Spend    Share

# Word Problems With LRDs (L$)

Momo has a L$5 bill and a L$10 bill. How much money does he have?

Papa gave Hawa a L$5 bill, a L$10 bill, and a L$20 bill. How much money does Hawa have?

Fatu has L$20. She buys a candy bar for L$5. How much money does she have left?

Korlu bought a keychain for L$10 and a book for L$20. How much money did she spend?

Momo has a L$10 bill and a L$20 bill. How much money does he have?

Mama gave Hawa 2 L$5 bills, a L$10 bill, and a L$20 bill. How much money does Hawa have?

Fatu has L$50. She buys a dress for L$20. How much money does she have left?

Momo gave Hawa L$5. Fatu give Hawa L$10. Korlu gave Hawa L$20. Mama gave Hawa L$5. How much money does Hawa have?

Papa took L$40 to the store with him. He spent L$10 on a pack of nails. How much money does Papa have now?

Mama took L$50 to the market with her. She spent L$10 on a bottle of palm oil and L$20 on a cup of rice. How much money does Mama have now?

Zaq took L$50 to the store with him. He spent L$10 on a pack of gum. How much money does Zaq have now?

Marie went to the bookstore. She purchased an eraser for L$5 and a pencil for L$10. How much money should she give the cashier?

# Social Studies

Map and Globe Skills
- Use cardinal directions
- Continents and Oceans
- Latitude and Longitude

Information Processing Skills
- Compare similarities and differences
- Organize items chronologically
- Identify issues and/or problems

Where We Live
- Explain that a map is a drawing of a place and a globe is a model of the earth
- Identify the city's geographic location in the world
- Model good citizenship
- Good behavior and habits
- Community Helpers and Workers

Personal Finance
- Currency and Money
- Explain that people must make choices because they cannot have everything they want
- Making smart decisions

Our Nation
- Counties, Capitals, and Flags
- Liberian Flag
- Pledge of Allegiance
- National Anthem
- Names of Presidents
- First and Current President
- Liberian Symbols
- Voting & Election

# Our Nation

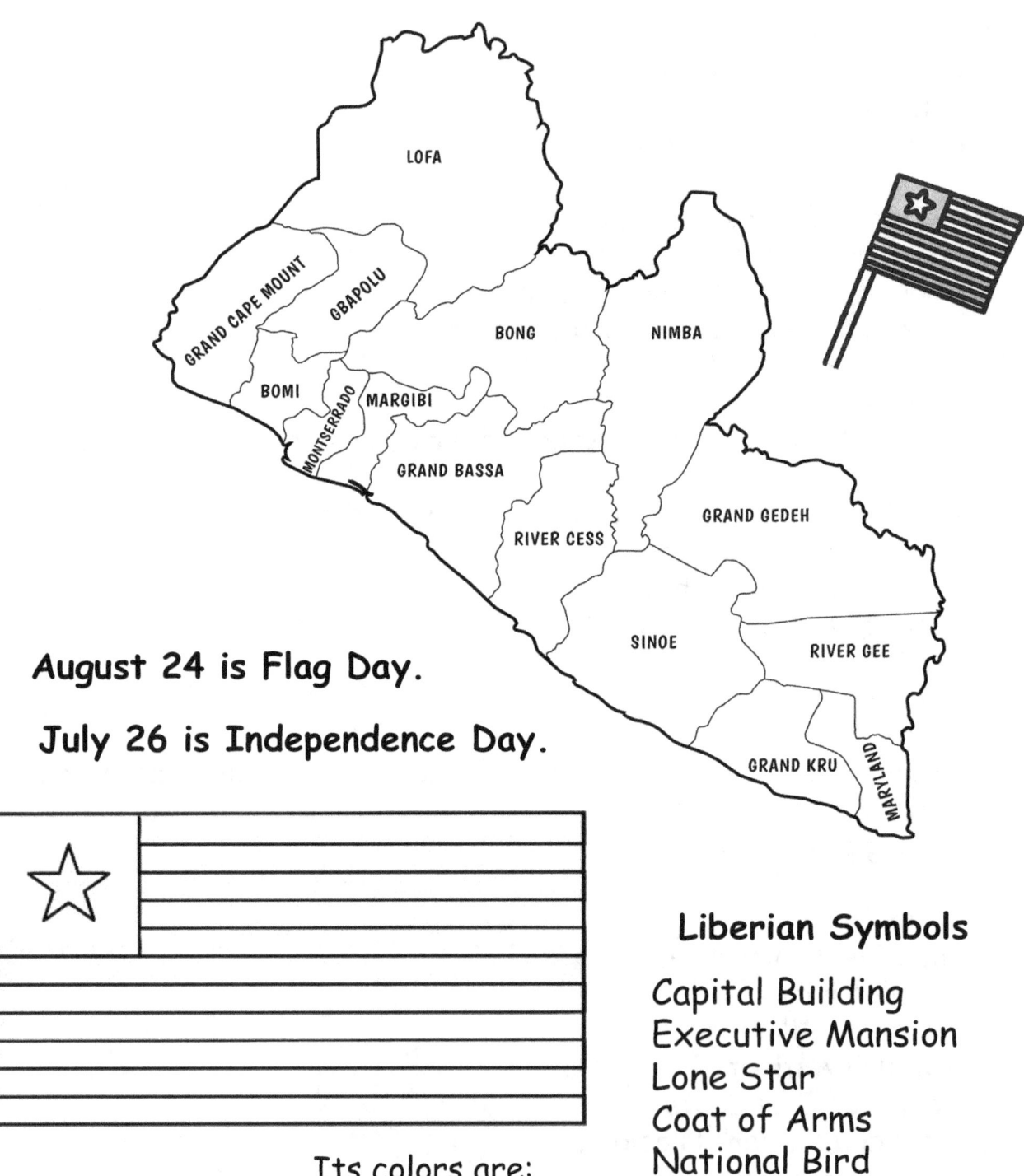

August 24 is Flag Day.

July 26 is Independence Day.

Our Flag

Its colors are:
Red, White and Blue

## Liberian Symbols

Capital Building
Executive Mansion
Lone Star
Coat of Arms
National Bird
Monrovia City Hall

# Liberia's Counties, Capitals, and Flags

**Bomi**
Tubmanburg

**Bong**
Gbarnga

**Gbarpolu**
Bopolu

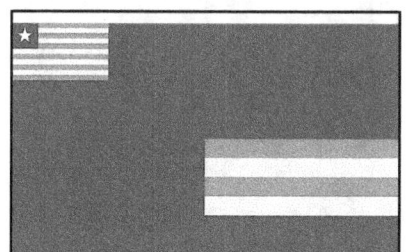
**Grand Bassa**
Buchanan

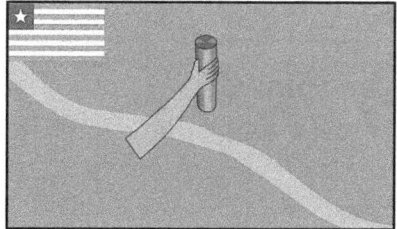
**Lofa**
Voinjama

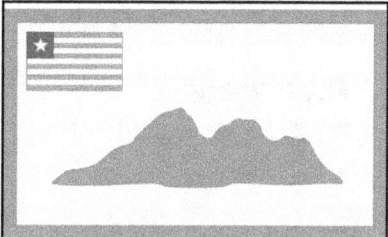
**Grand Cape Mount**
Robertsport

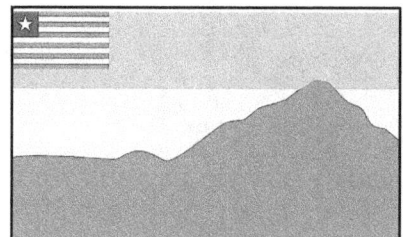
**Grand Gedeh**
Zwedru

**Grand Kru**
Barclayville

**Margibi**
Kakata

**Maryland**
Harper

**Montserrado**
Bensonville

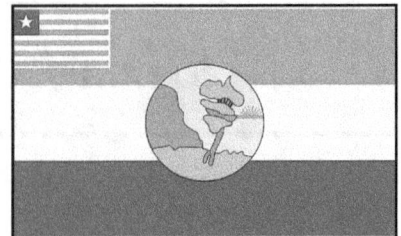
**Nimba**
Sanniquellie

**Rivercess**
Rivercess

**Sinoe**
Greenville

**River Gee**
Fish Town

Executive Mansion

# Names of Our Presidents

**George M. Weah**
President

**Jewel Howard-Taylor**
Vice President

Joseph J. Roberts
Stephen A. Benson
Daniel B. Warner
James S. Payne
Edward J. Roye
James S. Smith
Anthony W. Gardiner
Alfred F. Russell
Hilary R. W. Johnson
Joseph J. Cheeseman
William D. Coleman
Garretson W. Gibson
Arthur Barclay

Daniel E. Howard
Charles D. B. King
Edward J. Barclay
William V. S. Tubman
William R. Tolbert
Samuel K. Doe
Charles G. Taylor
Moses Blah
Ellen Johnson-Sirleaf
George Weah

# National Anthem

Lyrics by Daniel B. Warner, 1847
Music by Olmstead Luca, 1860

All Hail, Liberia Hail!
All Hail, Liberia Hail!
This glorious land of liberty
Shall long be ours.
Though new her name,
Green be for fame,
And mighty be her powers,

In joy and gladness
With our hearts united,
We'll shout the freedom
Of a race benighted,
Long live Liberia, happy land!
A home of glorious liberty,
By God's command!

All hail, Liberia, hail!
All hail, Liberia, hail!
In union strong success is sure
We cannot fail!
With God above
Our rights to prove
We will o'er all prevail,

With hearts and hands
Our country's cause defending

We'll meet the foe
With valor unpretending
Long live Liberia, happy land!
A home of glorious liberty,
By God's command!

# Who is a Patriot?

A patriot is a person who loves his or her country.

## What does a patriot do?

1. A patriot will stand and say the Pledge of Allegiance.
2. A patriot will salute his country's flag.
3. A patriot will hang up flags on Independence Day and Flag Day.
4. A patriot will wave the flag in a parade.
5. A patriot will wear red, white and blue.

I stand with my hand on my heart,
I pledge to the flag you see.
I love the red, white, and blue,
The land of liberty.

I pledge allegiance to the flag of Liberia,
and to the republic for which it stands,
one nation, indivisible, with liberty
and justice for all.

I promise to be loyal to the flag of Liberia,
and to the republic for which it stands,
one country under God, cannot be divided,
with freedom and fairness for all.

# Voting and Election

In Liberia, we have an election to vote for president and our leaders. The people who want to be the president or a leader are called candidates. Citizens make their choices for our leaders by using a ballot. In Liberia, we have the right to a secret ballot. That means we vote in private and don't have to share how we voted with anyone.

Your vote is your choice. Voting is a good way to be a part of big public decisions. During an election, every vote matters and every vote is counted.

A candidate is someone who wants your vote.

A debate is when different candidates explain why their idea is the best.

The ballot is a card with the candidates' pictures on it.

Explain the candidate names on the ballot. Give each student a ballot. Explain how to mark the ballot next to their choice. Remind students not to write his/her name on the ballot to keep the ballot secret. Fold the ballot in half when finished.

Show students the Ballot Box and explain its purpose. Have a helper pass around the Ballot Box so that each student can put his/her ballot into the box.

## How to Vote

First, learn everything about the candidates and their ideas when they debate. The candidates will debate on why their idea is better for Liberia. Listen to both sides and ask questions. The candidates will answer your questions to help you understand their plans.

Next, you will choose who you want to become president by using a ballot.

Last, you will mark an x on the candidate you choose.

Practical

## Let's Have an Election

1. Students will understand the process of voting through participation in a mock election activity.
2. The student will be able to explain why voting is a good way to make group decisions.

Materials Needed:
- Ballot Cards
- Election Tally Sheet
- Empty tissue box or container to hold ballots. Label empty tissue box or container with words "Ballot Box."

## Election Vote Tally

|  |  |
|---|---|
|  |  |

### Results Graph

| Candidate's Name |   |   |   |   |   |   |   |   |
|---|---|---|---|---|---|---|---|---|
| Candidate's Name |   |   |   |   |   |   |   |   |
|  | 1 | 2 | 3 | 4 | 5 | 6 | 7 | 8 |

**Learning Objectives** The student will be able to explain why voting is a good way to make group decisions.

1. Ask students, "What do we need to do if we want to find out who will win the election and be the president?" (Count the ballots)
2. Distribute Election Vote Tally Graph worksheet to each student.
3. Choose a helper to take the ballots out of the box one by one and read aloud which candidate got the mark on the ballot. The teacher or a reliable student volunteer will make a tally mark on the chalkboard to keep count of the votes as they are read. Direct students to make a mark on their worksheet, as modeled.
4. When finished, count up the tallies and determine who won the election. Have students complete graph using data from the election tally.

Discuss "Why is voting a good way to make decisions?"

# Rules and Laws

## Rules

Rules and laws are made to keep us happy and safe.

Rules are made for people to follow at certain times.

Walking in a line can be a rule for students at school.

Doing your homework before going out to play can be a rule for kids at home.

What rule do you have to follow?

## Laws

Laws are a little different. They are for all people to follow at all times.

Driving with the speed limit is a law for all drivers.

Putting litter in the trash is a law for all people.

People who follow rules and laws make our world happy and safe.

# Currency & Money

| LRD (S) & USD ($) |

Currency includes coins and paper bills.
A penny is worth 1¢. A nickle is worth 5¢.
A dime is worth 10¢. A quarter is worth 25¢.

## What Can We Do With Our Money?

SAVE for emergencies
SUPPLY our needs
SPEND on our wants
SHARE with other people in need

## Making Smart Decisions

People cannot have everything they want, they have to make choices. You have to choose things you need to live (food, clothes, a house) and things that you want (toys, candy, a bike).

Needs come before Wants! First spend money on what you need. Then you can spend money on what you want.

Have students make two lists; things people need to live and things people want.

Ask students to name one thing they would like to have. In order to get what they want, they will have to ....

148

# Community Helpers & Volunteers

## Community Helpers

| | | | |
|---|---|---|---|
| Judge | Baker | Babysitter | Surgeon |
| Taxi Driver | Painter | Mailman | Detective |
| Writer | Nurse | Mechanic | Garbage Collector |
| Dentist | Detective | Scientist | Flight Attendant |
| Janitor | Librarian | Vet | Internet Technologist |
| Police | Lawyer | Banker | Market Woman |
| Firefighter | Cashier | Waiter | Bank Teller |
| Coach | Astronaut | Hairstylist | Meteorologist |
| Teacher | Doctor | Chef | Pharmacist |
| Plumber | Pilot | Bus Driver | Forest Ranger |
| Carpenter | Scientist | Paramedic | Photographer |
| Soldier | Lifeguard | Pro Athlete | Volunteer |
| Reporter | Musician | Farmer | |

Discuss the role of each community helper. Do dramatic play for each community helper.

What community helper would you like to be when you grow up?
Why?

### How can we be a great citizen in our community?
1. Say I'm sorry... everybody makes mistakes.
2. Care about others. Treat them nicely.
3. Do what is right. Say what is true.
4. Invite others to participate.
5. Do the work you are supposed to do.
6. Say and do nice things for others.
7. Control what you say and do.
8. Help others.

# Volunteering

Volunteering means spending some of your free time helping others. You can volunteer to help other people, but you can also volunteer to protect animals, the environment, or anything that you care about, like Sapo National Park in Sinoe County.

## Why Become a Volunteer?

Volunteering helps you make new friends.
Volunteering makes you happy.
Volunteering helps you believe in yourself.
Volunteering makes you proud.
Volunteering makes you feel good about yourself.
Volunteering helps you do good for others in the community.

## What volunteers can do.

1. Volunteers collect food for those who don't have anything to eat.
2. Volunteers help old people.
3. Volunteers help to protect the environment by planting trees and picking up trash.
4. Volunteers donate their blood to help doctors save lives.
5. Volunteers teach the class when teachers are not well to teach.
6. Volunteers visit sick people to help them feel better.
7. Volunteers also protect the animals at Monkey Island and Sapo National Park.

Students can list other things volunteers can do at home and in the community.

# Science - Smart Start

## Characteristics of Science

- Science and Scientists
- Discuss the importance of curiosity, honesty, openness, and skepticism in science and exhibit these traits in efforts to understand how the world works.
- Demonstrate knowledge of scientific processes and inquiry methods.
- Apply computation and estimation skills necessary for analyzing data and following scientific investigations.
- Use tools and instruments for observing, measuring, and manipulating objects in scientific activities.
- Use the concepts of system, model, change, and scale when exploring scientific and technological matters.
- Communicate scientific ideas and activities clearly.
- Weather

Earth Science
- Analyze time patterns and objects (sun, moon, stars) in the day and night sky.
- Describe the physical attributes of rocks and soils.
- Landforms

Physical Science
- States of Matter
- Describe objects in terms of their composition and physical attributes.
- Explore the forces that cause a change in motion (speed and direction, push and pull)
- Observe and communicate the effect of gravity on objects.

Energy Science
- Electrical Energy
- Elastic Energy

- Kinetic Energy
- Chemical Energy
- Sound Energy
- Light Energy
- Muscle Energy
- Energy sources, need energy to live, energy chain, human energy chain
- Natural Energy
- Renewable Energy, solar, wind, hydroelectric plant, plants, animals
- Non-renewable Energy; gasoline, natural gas, iron ore, oil
- How we use energy in our lives; power station, hydro, battery, airplane, car, traffic light, fan, fire

Life Science
- Plants and Animals
- Distinguish living things from non-living things based on physical attributes.
- Compare and contrast groups of organisms.
- Our body
- Our five senses – sight, hearing, touch, smell, and taste

Healthy Habits
- Bathroom Rules
- Hand washing steps
- Healthy Habits
- Prevent Malaria

# Science and Scientists

What is science? Science is the study of our world around us. A Scientist is someone who studies how a specific thing works.

## Different Areas of Science

Human and Animal Life

Plant

The Earth

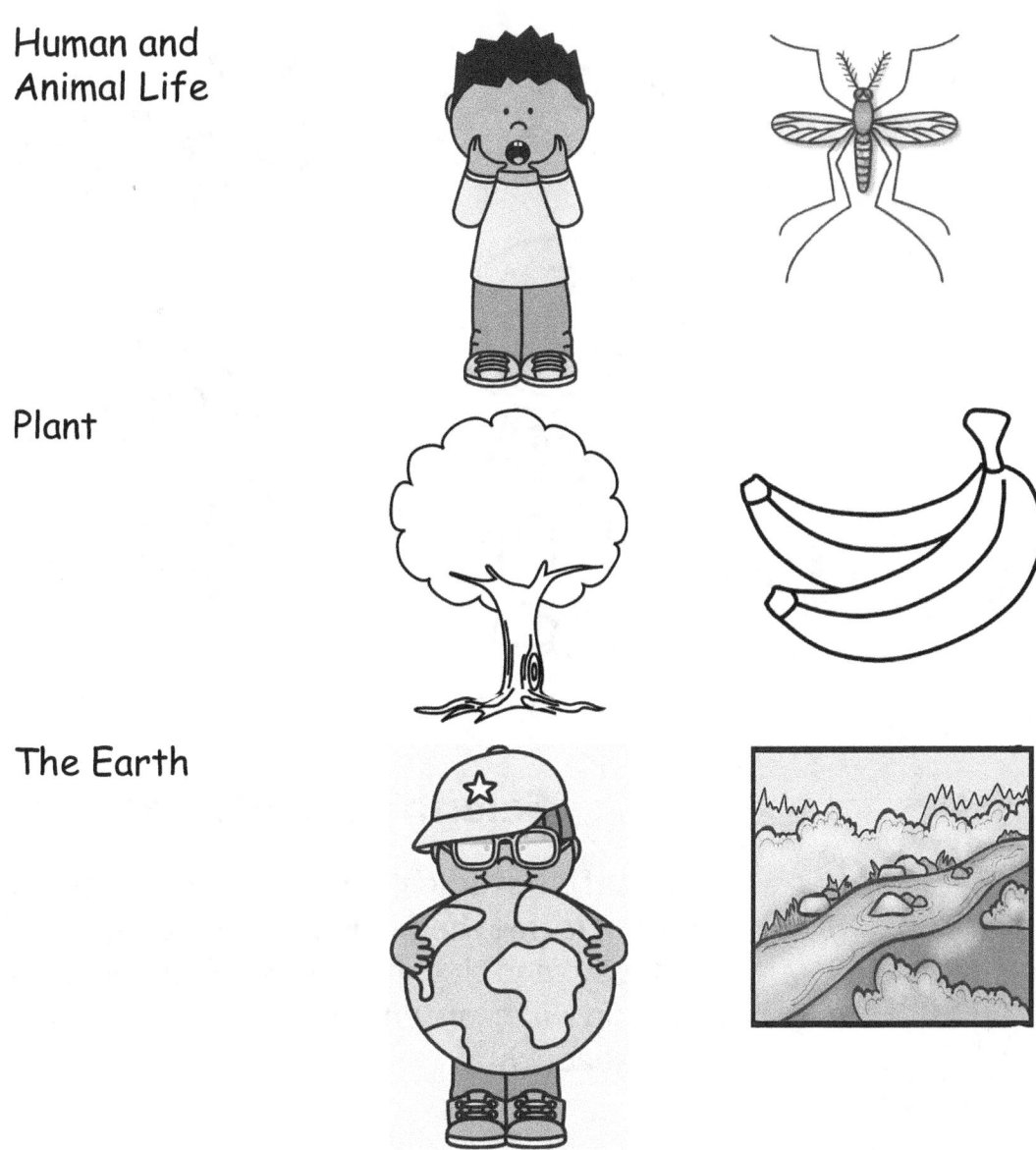

The Environment

Energy and Motion

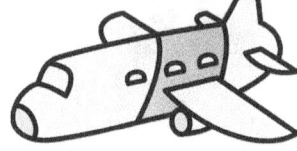 

Outer Space

## Scientific Methods

A Scientist studies how a specific thing works. **Scientific methods** are steps scientists take to study and learn things. This helps them come up with an answer. What do scientists do? Research!

# Scientist Activities

Research
- they ask a question
- they form a hypothesis (guess)
- they test and experiment
- they record their observation
- they come to a conclusion

## Scientists' Tools & Instruments

|  |  |
|---|---|
|  | microscope |
|  | magnet |
|  | beaker |
|  | magnifying glass |

|  | balance |
|---|---|

## Weather Measurement Tools

|  |  |
|---|---|
|  | **thermometer** - an instrument for measuring temperature. |
|  | **rain gauge** - an instrument for measuring the quality of water that falls to earth; rain, snow, hail. |
|  | **wind sock** - shows the direction of the wind. |
|  | **weather vane** - shows which way the wind is blowing. |

| 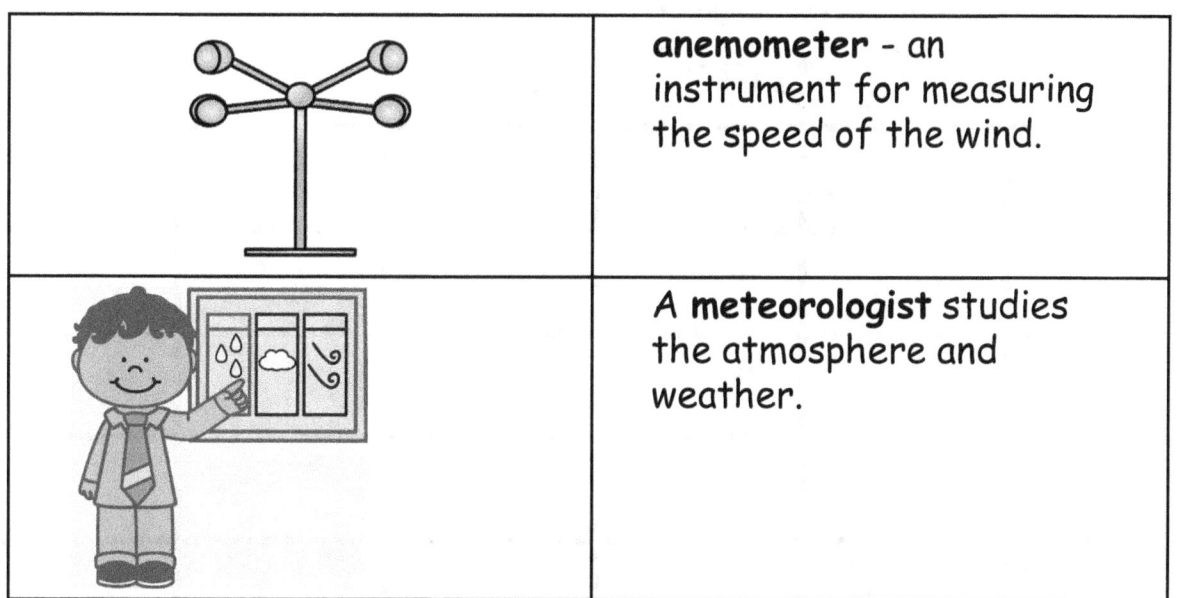 | **anemometer** - an instrument for measuring the speed of the wind. |
| --- | --- |
| | A **meteorologist** studies the atmosphere and weather. |

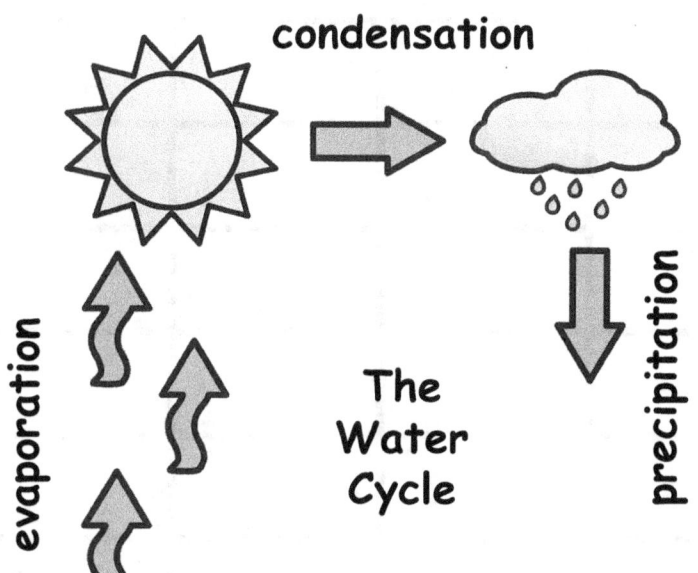

condensation - conversion of a vapor to liquid.

precipitation - water that falls to the earth as rain or snow.

evaporation - to change into vapor.

accumulation - an act of collecting or garthering.

Have class track the weather for one week during the rainy season & one week during the dry season.

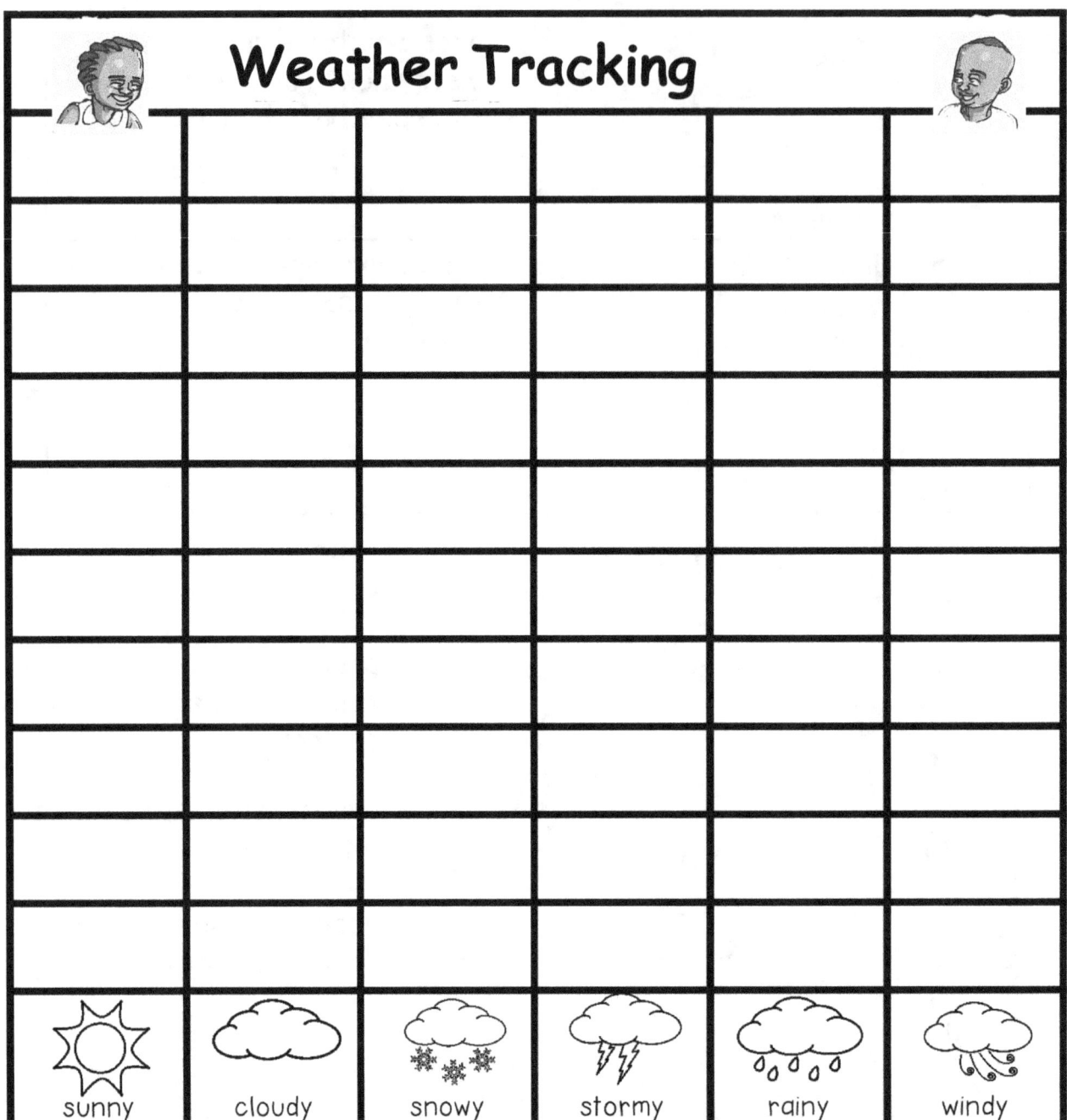

**Weather in Liberia**

**Rainy Season**
May to October

**Dry Season**
November to April

How many days were sunny?
How many days were snowy?
How many days were cloudy?
How many days were windy?
How many days were rainy?
How many days were stormy?

# Earth Science

Earth sciences involve the study of everything relating to the Earth, except for living things. These sciences include mainly geology and meteorology, although for some it would also include geography.

We love our planet Earth, so we must protect it all year round. On Earth Day, we honor the earth and celebrate. We should recycle cans, plastic, and paper by putting them in a bin that has a recycling symbol on it. Everyone can recycle to keep it neat and clean. We can prevent extra trash by adding biodegradable items (to break down into very small harmless parts by the action of living things) to a compost bin outside our home. Most biodegradable items are food waste from the kitchen.

We celebrate Earth Day on April 22nd each year. Some people celebrate Earth Day by planting a tree, plant, or flower. You can do this in your own backyard with the help of an adult. Help clean up the earth with your family and friends!

### Earth's Layers
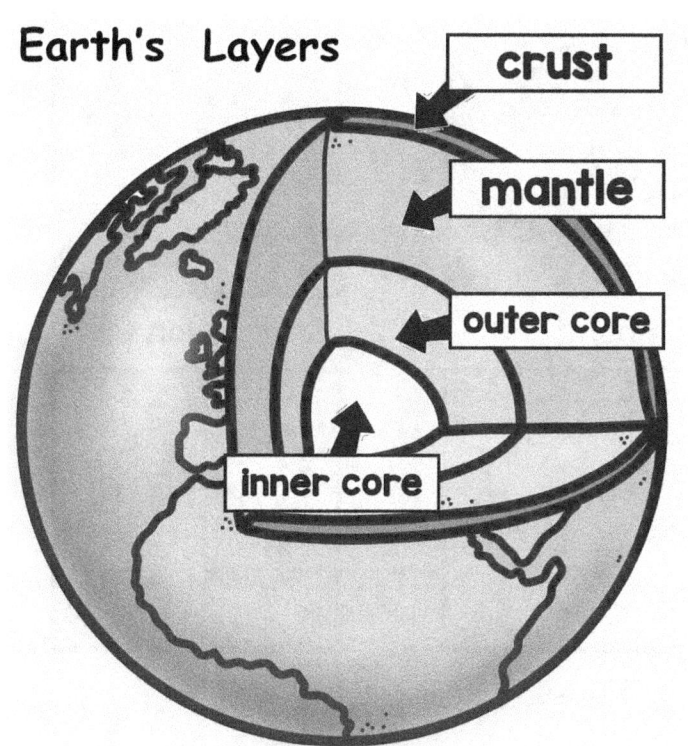

### Earth's Composition

Earth Day is April 22nd. How are you going to celebrate this year?

## Types of Soil

clay

silt

sand

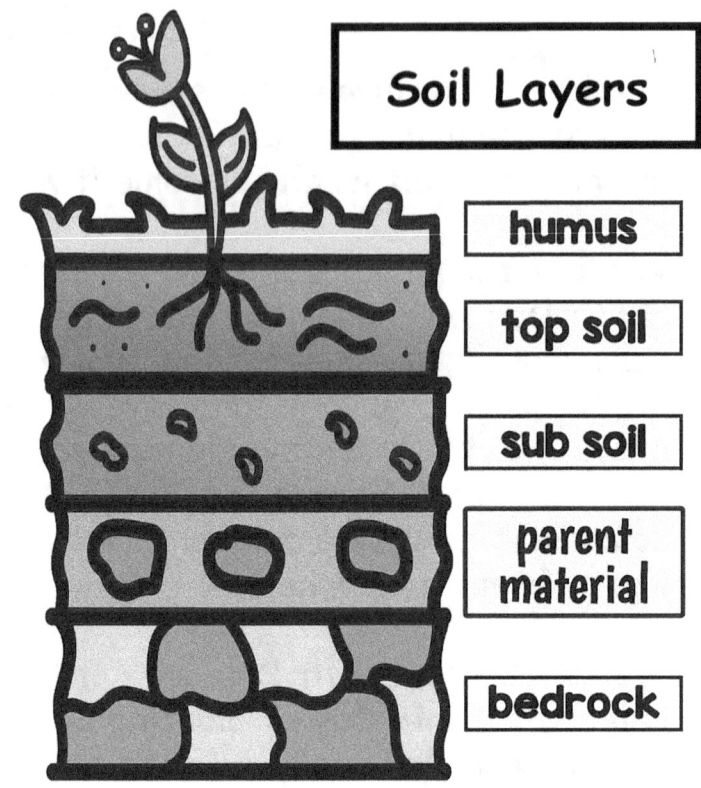

## Soil Layers

humus

top soil

sub soil

parent material

bedrock

## The 12 types of landform

mountains

pond

canyon

cave

island

river

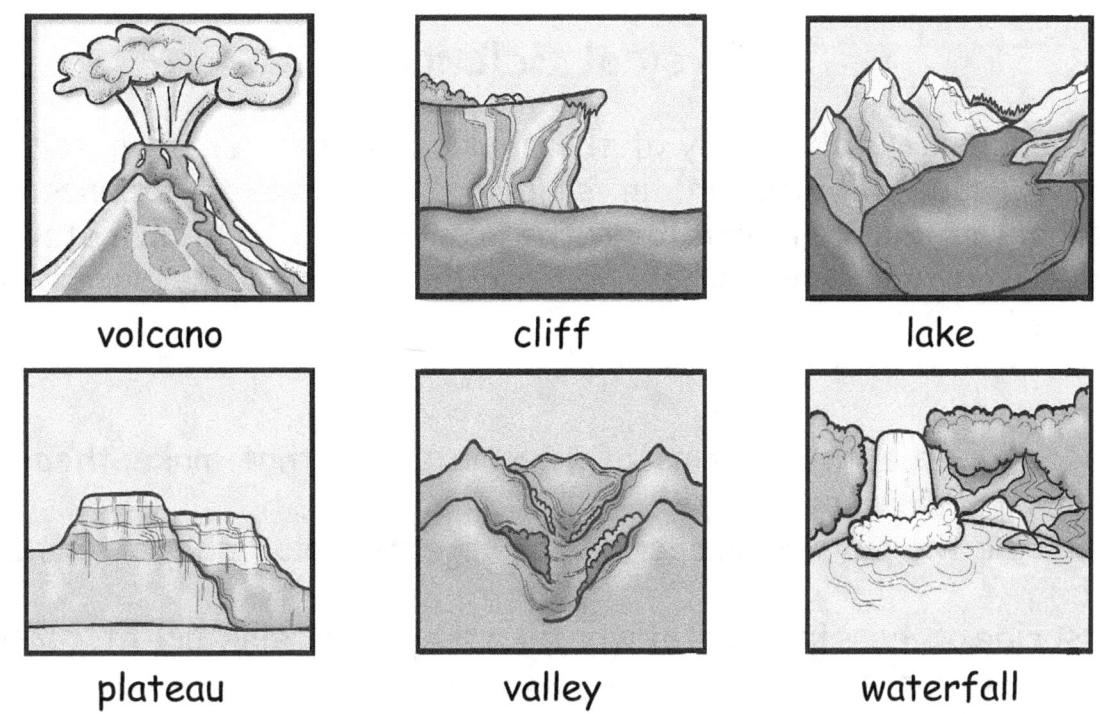

## Landforms in Liberia

### Mountains
Mount Wuteve
Wologisi
Bong Range

### Lakes
Lake Piso

### Waterfalls
Wongan
Kpatawee

### Rivers
Lofa River
Mano River
Mesurado
Farmington River
St. Paul
Cavalla
St. John

### Islands
Bushrod Island
Providence Island
Bali Island

# Physical Science

Physical science is the study of the physical properties of materials. Generally speaking, though, in studying the physical sciences in kindergarten, children learn about the properties of certain materials and discover that these properties can be observed, measured, and predicted.

Students will:
- Describe objects in terms of the materials that make them up (cloth, paper, wood, etc.)
- Describe the physical properties of objects (color, shape, texture, etc.)
- Describe objects in terms of whether they float, sink, are attracted to magnets, etc.
- Recognize the properties of water — it can be a liquid or solid and can change back and from one to the other, and it can evaporate when left in an open container.
- Recognize that light and heat are both sources of energy.

| States of Matter | | |
|---|---|---|
| Solid | Liquid | Gas |
| wood | milk | fire |
| things that float | things that sink | things that are soft |
| feather<br>boat | rock<br>iron | pillow<br>t-shirt |
| things that are light | things that are rough | things that are heavy |
| balloon<br>bag | broom<br>rope | bus<br>elephant |

# Simple Machines

A simple machine is a device that can change the direction or the magnitude of a force, or the point where it is applied. This is done so that the force can be used to do work.

Simple machines are used to make Big machines. There are six basic types of simple machines: wheel & axle, pulley, lever, inclined plane, wedge and screw.

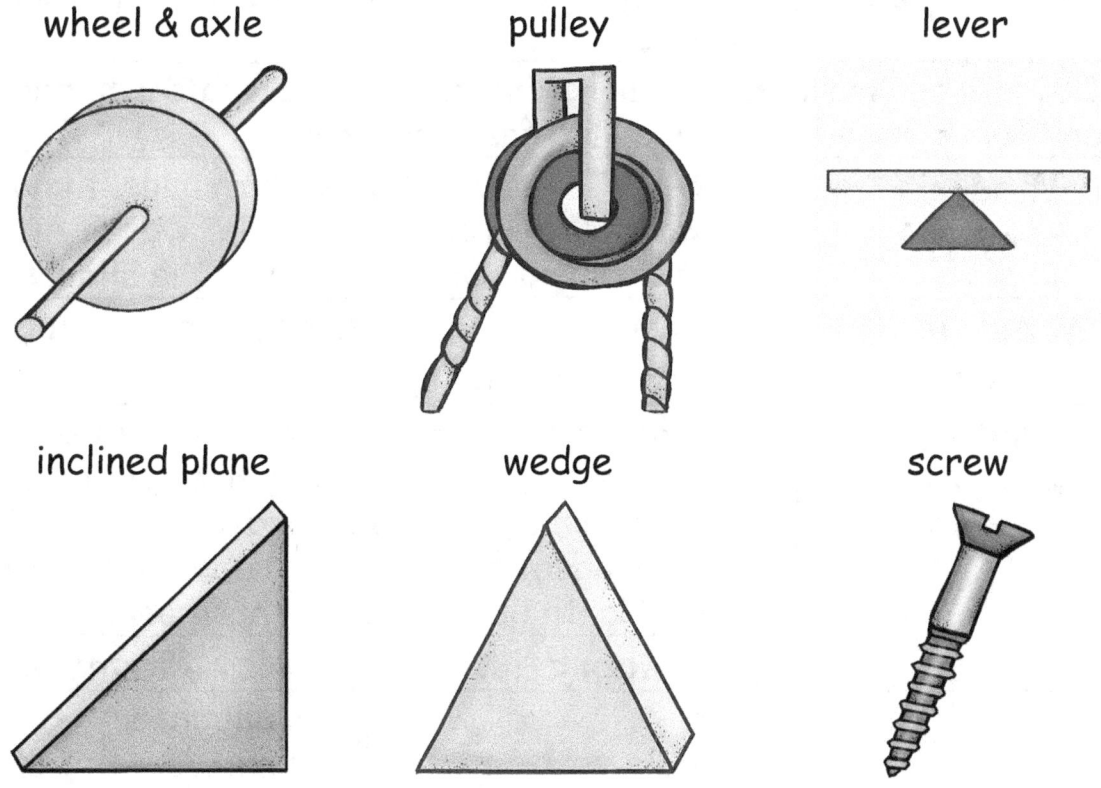

Simple machines have been helping people to do work for thousands of years! The lever, wheel and axle, pulley, inclined plane, wedge, and screw, each have a job to do. Some amplify force, some change its direction, and some reduce friction or create mechanical advantage.

## Force & Motion

How do things move?

> By force.

**FORCE** is a **push** or **pull** that may make something move.

| What is speed? | SPEED is how quickly or slowly something moves. |
|---|---|
| Objects can move in a straight line, zig zag, up and down, back and forth, round and round, and fast and slow. ||
| What is gravity? | GRAVITY is the force that pulls things toward the ground. Example, water in a waterfall flow or sliding down the slide. |
| What is a ramp? | A ramp is a slanting surface connecting a lower level to a higher level. |
| What is a magnet? | A magnet is an object that attracts some kinds of metals. A magnet has two poles. The poles are at each end of a magnet. Each magnet has a north pole and a south pole. North poles attract south poles. |
| | **Magnetic** — can, needle, nails, pin    **Not Magnetic** — highlighter, shell, paper, t-shirt |

Students can bring six magnetic objects and six non-magnetic objects.

# Energy Science

Energy is something that is needed to make things happen.

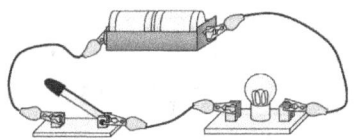
**Electrical Energy**

**Elastic Energy**

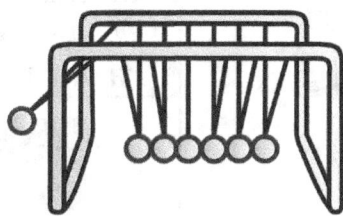
**Kinetic Energy**

**Chemical Energy**

**Muscle Energy**

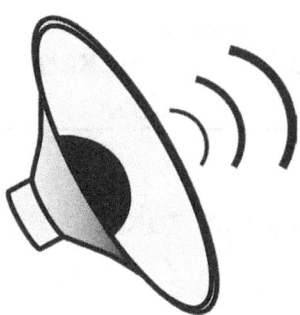
**Sound Energy**

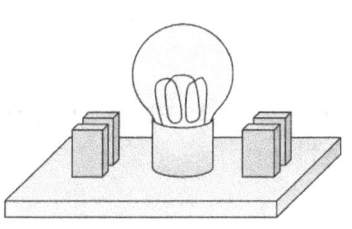
**Light Energy**

**Energy Sources**

**Where do we get our energy from?**
The most important source of enegry is the Super Duper Sun. (Warmth, Light, Energy, Power, Life, Food)

What would the Earth be like if there was no sun? What would happen to plants, animals, and people?

## We Need Energy To Live

| We get energy from the sun. | We get energy from animals. | We get energy from plants. |
|---|---|---|
| Playing outside. | Chicken<br>Cow | Rice<br>Cassava |

**Energy Chain** is the path energy takes to get from one living thing to another.

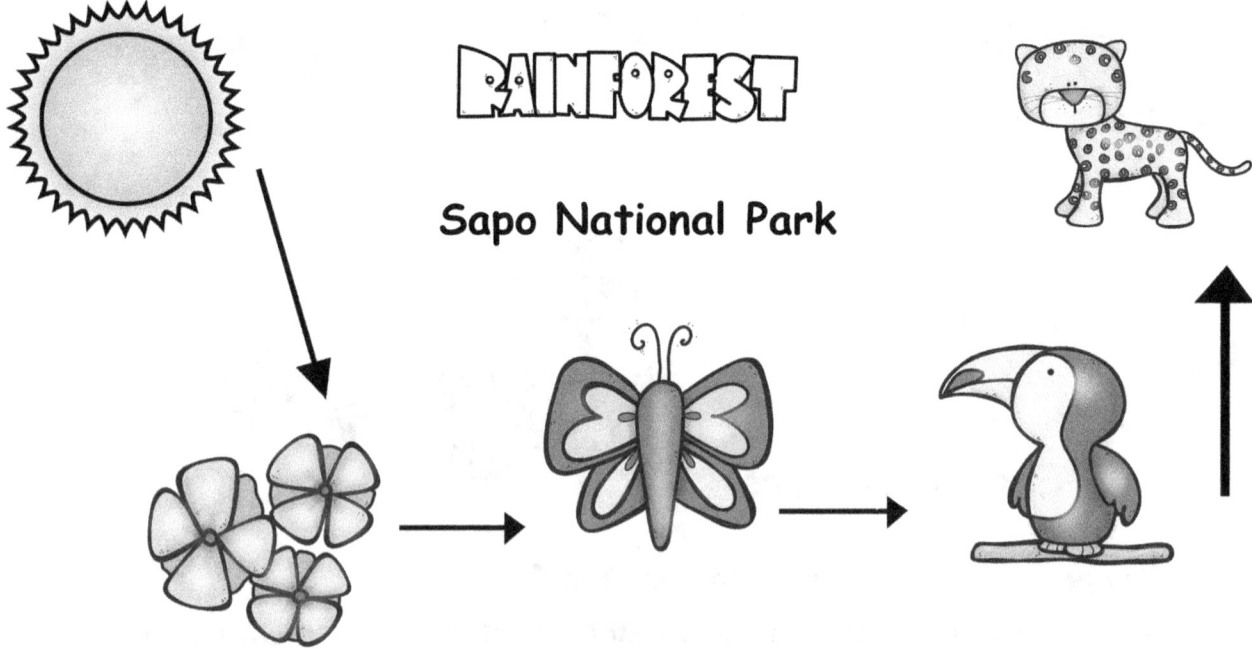

Sapo National Park

Discuss the human energy chain.

166

# Natural Energy Resources

Nature provides us with energy in the form of natural resources. Natural resources can be living or nonliving. Not all natural resources last forever. There are 2 different types of natural energy sources.

**WIND** **RENEWABLE energy** **wave**
**BIOMASS**
**SOLAR** **GEOTHERMAL** **tidal**

Renewable energy resources can be replaced. They are produced by nature again and again.

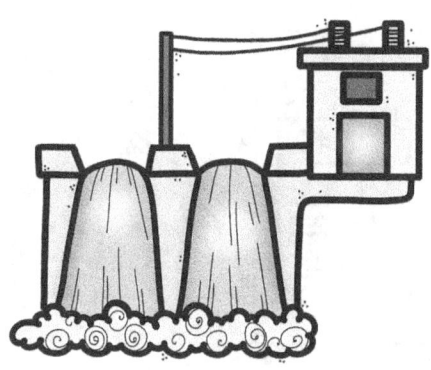

**Solar**
Energy from the sun changed to electricity.

**Wind**
Energy from wind changed to electricity

**Hydroelectric Power**
Energy from a waterfall flow changed to electricity.

## Renewable Energy

**Plants**
Energy in the form of food.

**Animals**
Energy in the form of food for other animals and humans.

## Non-renewable Energy

Non-renewable energy resources cannot be replaced in our lifetime. They take thousands, even millions, of years to replace.

Gasoline        Natural Gas        Iron Ore        Oil

*fossil fuels — decayed plants and animals that have been changed to oil, coal, and natural gas

# How We Use Energy

Energy in our lives.

Power Station

Hydro

Battery

Airplane

Car

Traffic Light

Fan

Fire

Microphone

Discuss other ways we use energy around the house.

# Life Science
## Living vs Non-living

Animals, plants, and people are living. They need three things to survive: food, water, and air.

food    water    air

**Nonliving things** do not grow. They do not need food, water, or air.

**Living things** grow. They need food, water, or air.

# Man-made Vs. Natural

| Man-made | Natural |
|---|---|
|  |  |
| 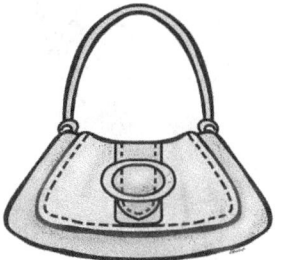 |  |
|  |  |
|  |  |

## Gifts of the sun

The sun gives us heat. Without the heat from the sun, we would not be able to survive on Earth. Plants use the sun to grow and help make food.

The sun gives us light. Light helps us to see during the day.

Things that protect us from the sun.

food

# Plants

Plants are living organisms. They create and use energy, grow, and release oxygen. Plants use water, air, minerals, nutrients and sunlight to live.

**Roots** - The roots of a plant are what hold the plant into the ground. They are hair-like and white in color. Roots soak up water and nutrients from the soil like a sponge

**Stem** - The stem of a plant holds the plant upright. The stem is usually green and cylinder-shaped like a straw. The stem carries water and nutrients, up and down, and to other parts of the plant.

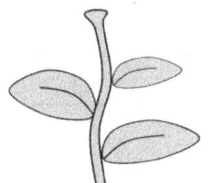

**Leaves** - The leaves of a plant help to make energy for the plant. Leaves also have veins to carry food and water to and from the stem. Leaves use sunlight, water, and air to create energy for the plant.

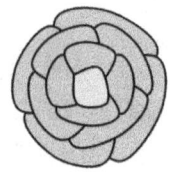

**Flower** - The flower of a plant makes the seeds. The flower is colorful and smells good to attract insects. Flowers also create nectar to attract insects. Insects help spread the pollen from the flower.

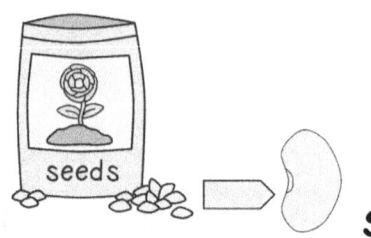
**Seeds**

The flower of a plant makes the seeds. Seeds begin the cycle of that same plant all over again. Seeds can travel by wind, animals, and water.

## Eating Plants

| When we eat | When we eat | When we eat |
|---|---|---|
| **eddos** | **onions** | **okra** |
| We are eating the | We are eating the | We are eating the |
| **root** | **stem** | **flower** |
| | | |
| When we eat | When we eat | |
| **potato greens** | **corn** | |
| We are eating the | We are eating the | |
| **leaves** | **seeds** | |
| | | |

Have students bring a rooted plant and identify parts of a plant.

# Life Cycle of Plants

All plants grow and change. A plant begins its life inside of a seed. Soon it sprouts from the seed and rises from the soil as a seedling. Finally, the seedling will grow and change into a full grown plant.

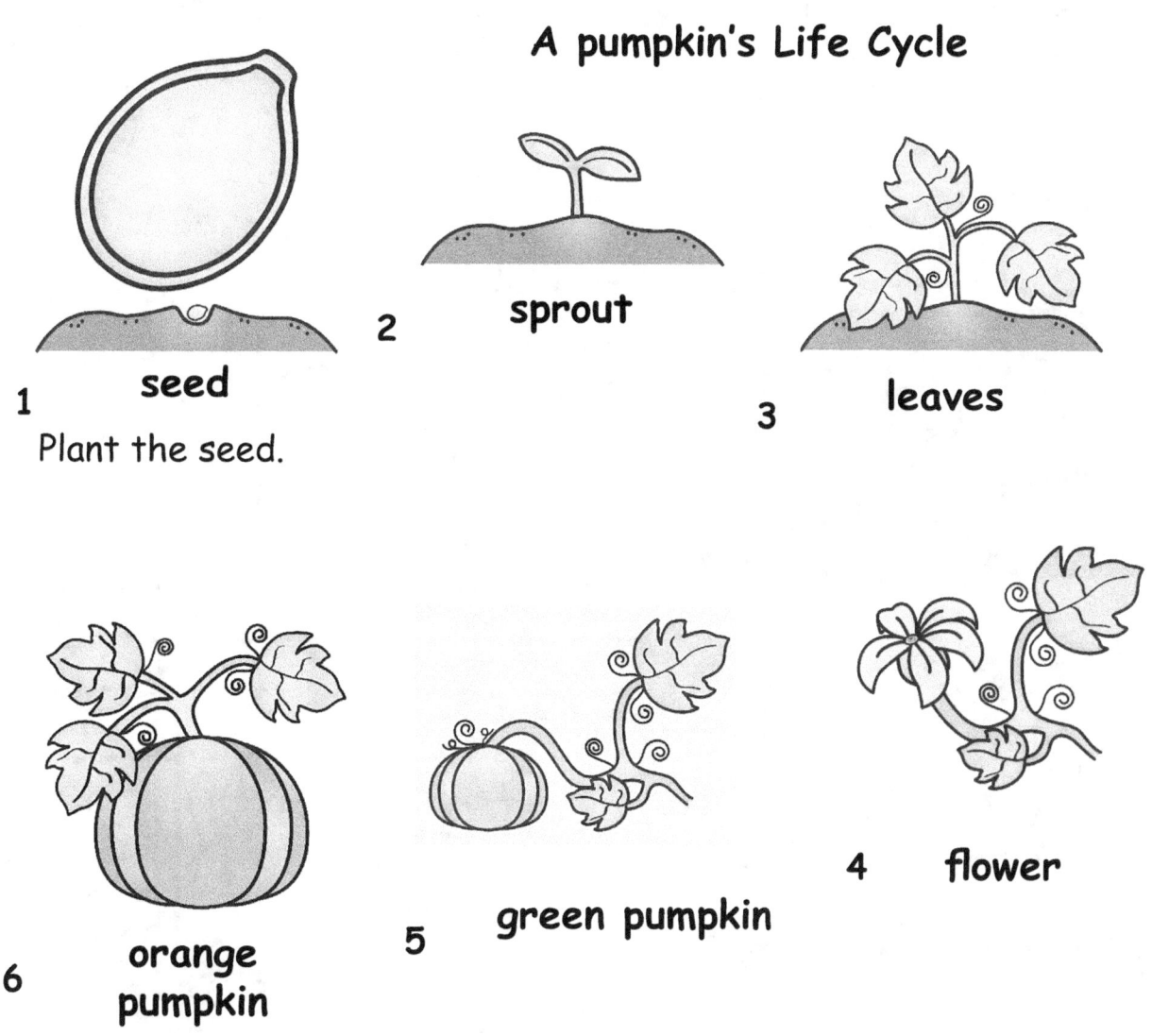

A pumpkin's Life Cycle

1 seed
Plant the seed.

2 sprout

3 leaves

4 flower

5 green pumpkin

6 orange pumpkin

# Plants in Our Lives

# Animals

An animal is a living thing (like earthworms, crabs, birds, and people) that is different from plants, being able to move about and depend on plants and animals for food.

## Animal characteristics

| These animals live on a farm. | These animals have a tail. | These animals have feathers. |
|---|---|---|
| chicken<br>cow<br>goat | monkey<br>dog<br>hippo | duck<br>owl<br>pepper bird |
| **These animals live in the forest.** | **These animals have scales.** | **These animals have Fur.** |
| lion<br>giraffe<br>deer | fish<br>lizard<br>snake | rabbit<br>fox<br>horse |
| | **Animal Movement** | |
| **Some animals hop.** | **Some animals fly.** | **Some animals swim.** |
| grasshopper<br>frog<br>rabbit | mosquito<br>bee<br>bird | fish<br>octopus<br>alligator |

# Animal Babies Grow Up

| calf | cow | chick | chicken |

| foal | horse | lamb | sheep |

| piglet | pig | kid | goat |

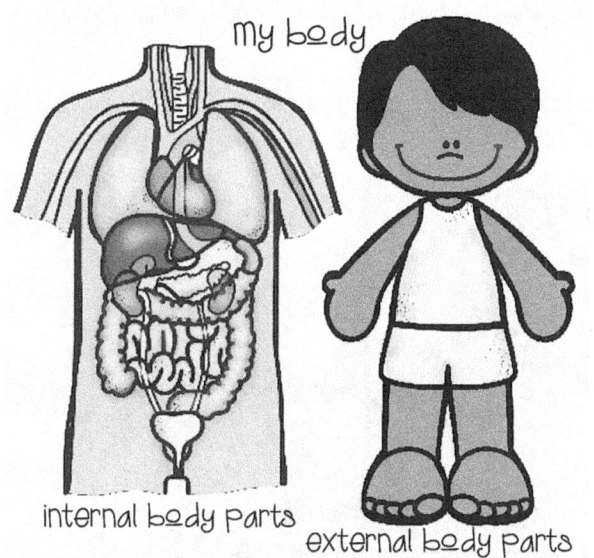

## Our Body

The bones in my body make up my skeleton. My skeleton gives me shape. It protects the soft part inside me. I have over 200 bones.

| **blood** | **bones** | **skeleton** |

The muscles help me move by pulling the bones in my body. The best way to keep my muscles strong is to exercise everyday.

| **oxygen** | **muscles** | **lungs** |

My heart and lungs work together. When I breathe in, my lungs take in oxygen. Oxygen goes into my blood. Then my heart pumps the blood to all the different parts of my body.

| **spine** | **brain** | **nerves** |

My brain keeps my body alive. It helps me move and think. It tells my nerves what to do. These nerves go down my spine to each part of my body. My body works because of my brain.

# My Body

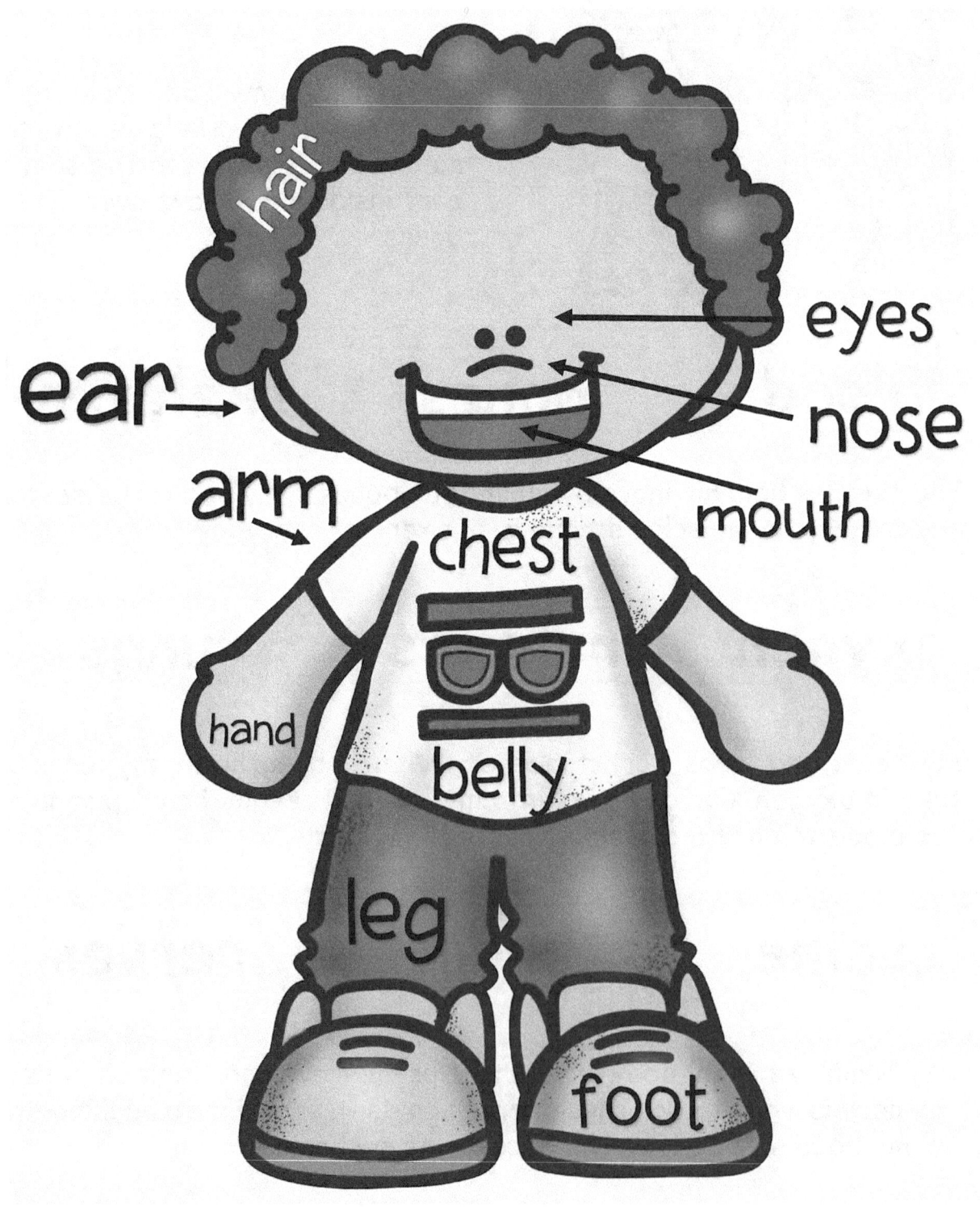

## Our Five Senses

We explore the world using our five senses.

| | | |
|---|---|---|
| **touch** | (hand) | I touch and feel things |
| **hearing** | (ear) | I hear with my ears. |
| **smell** | (nose) | I smell with my nose. |
| **sight** | (eye) | I see with my eyes. |
| **taste** | (mouth) | The taste buds on my tongue let me enjoy my favorite foods. |

# Human Growth Stages

## Human Life Cycle sequencing

Rearrange and help students practice putting the human growth stages in order.

young baby   baby   toddler   young child

child   teen   young adult   midage

oldage

Baby Stage - Babies rely on adults to care for them. Babies spend a lot of time sleeping and eating. Baby drink milk and are learning to crawl.

Child Stage - Children still rely on adults to care for them. Children can do more things on their own, like walking and going to school. Children can eat more types of foods.

# Human Growth Stages

Teenager Stage - Teenagers can drive and have jobs. Teenagers enjoy a variety of activities. Teenagers sleep and eat a lot, as they are growing and becoming like adults.

young baby    baby    toddler    young child

child    teen    young adult    midage

oldage

Adult Stage - Adults go to work to make money. Adults must take care of their children. Adults are always very busy, and don't sleep as much as children or teenagers.

Elderly person Stage - Elderly people are old and very tired. Elderly people sleep a lot and eat softer foods. Elderly people enjoy activities like visiting and spending time with their relatives and friends.

**Mosquito bites make us sick with Malaria.**

## Life Cycle of a Mosquito

The full life-cycle of a mosquito takes about a month. They go through four stages of development. The four stages are egg, pupa, larva, and adult. The adult lives for only a few weeks.

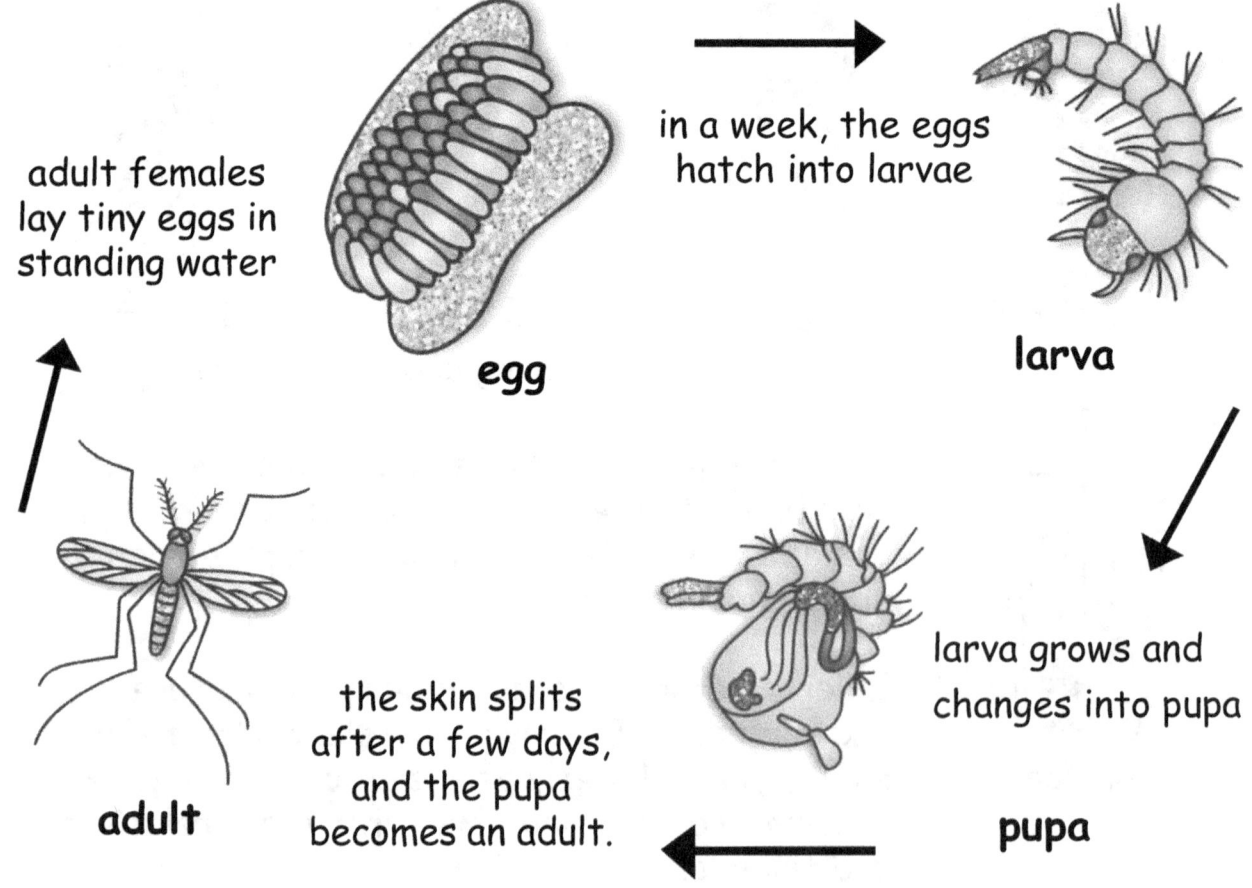

How to prevent malaria and stay well.

Always keep your home and yard clean of garbage.

Get anti-malaria medicine from your doctor.

Do not keep dirty water around.

Use mosquito net and spray to prevent bites.

# Hand Washing Steps

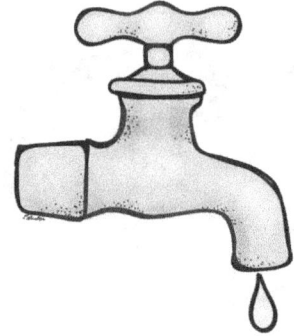
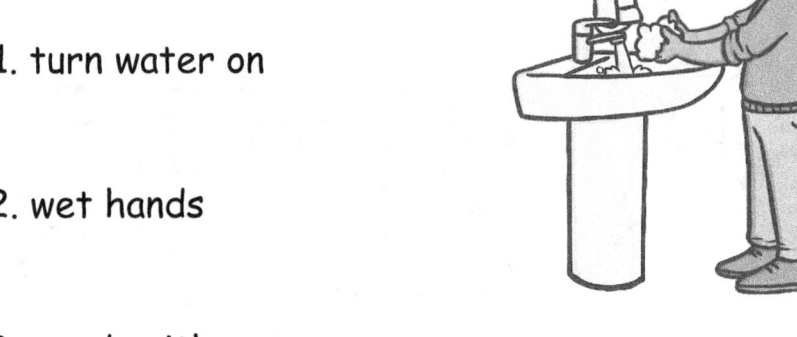

1. turn water on

2. wet hands

3. scrub with soap

4. rinse clean

5. dry hands

6. put paper towel in trash

**Things we can do during the day.**

Look at a rainbow
go to school
ride a bike
play at the beach

**Things we can do during the night.**

sleep
catch lightning bugs
look at the stars
use a flashlight

# Healthy Habits

## Bathroom Rules

# Technology

Accessing Information / Reference Skills
- Explore the use of the media center, picture books, audiovisual resources, and available technology for reading and writings.
- Technology word list.

Computers
- What is a computer?
- Desktop and Laptop.
- Parts of a computer.
- Types of devices.

Online Digital Safety
- Staying safe online, protecting Private Information (name, address, phone number, email, address, school)
- Using Technology in Solving Problems.
- Things made by humans to make life easier and help solve problems.

Technology at Home and School
- Media Centers.
- Making Connections.

Comparing Technology
- Technology Then and Now.

Technology in Transportation
- Carrying people or goods from one place to another.
- Travel by land, air, and water.
- Travel far and fast.

# Computer

## Learning to use the computer.

A computer is a device used for working with information. These skills will help you to develop your learning through the use of technology.

The printer lets you print information from the computer onto paper. You can do your schoolwork using a computer.

## Student's Goal

1. turn on a computer and login.
2. use the keyboard to type.
3. use a mouse or finger to move pictures and click on things.
4. use icons and menus to open programs.
5. work with tablets.
6. do school work on a smartboard.
7. explain the rules about using devices the right way.
8. know the consequences of not using devices appropriately.

# Desktop Computer

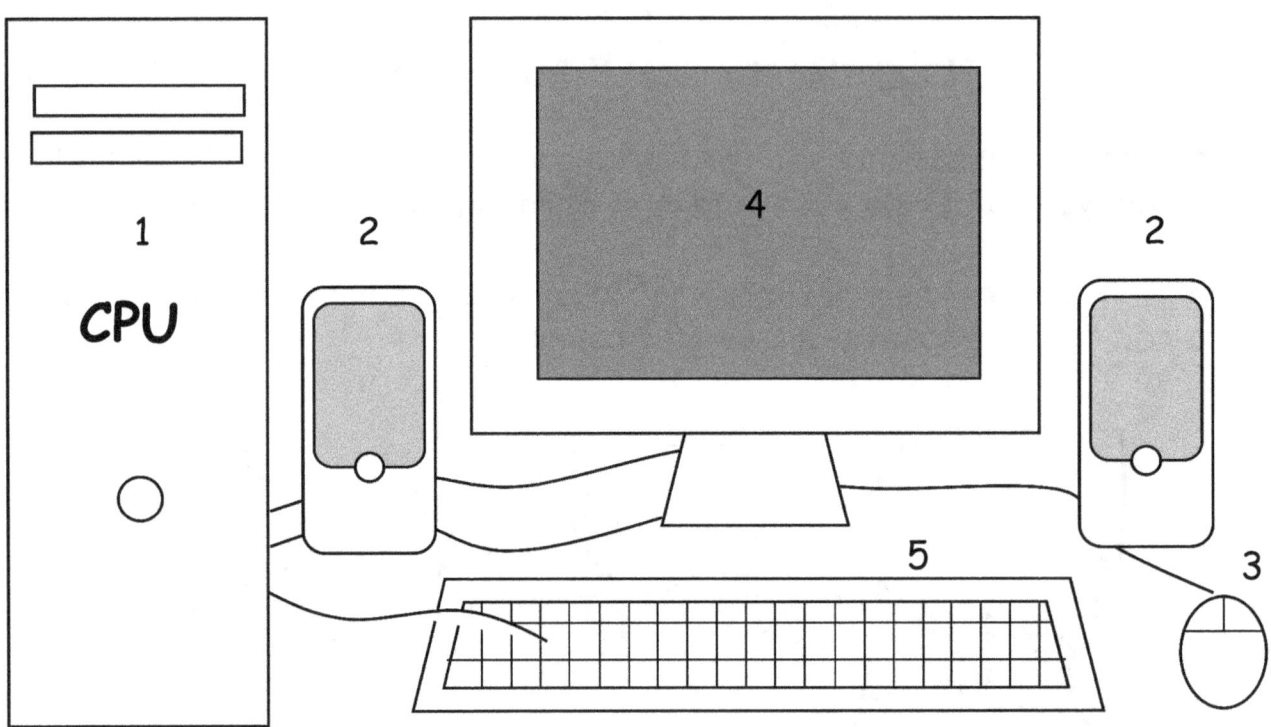

**1** The CPU is the "brain" of the computer. It processes information.

**2** The speakers play any sounds that come from the computer. They are an **output** device.

**4** The monitor is the display of the computer. It shows information for me to see.
It is an **output** device.

mouse

**3** The mouse allows me to move the cursor and click. It is an **input** device.

**5** The keyboard allows me to type information into the computer. It is an **input** device.

# Laptop Computer

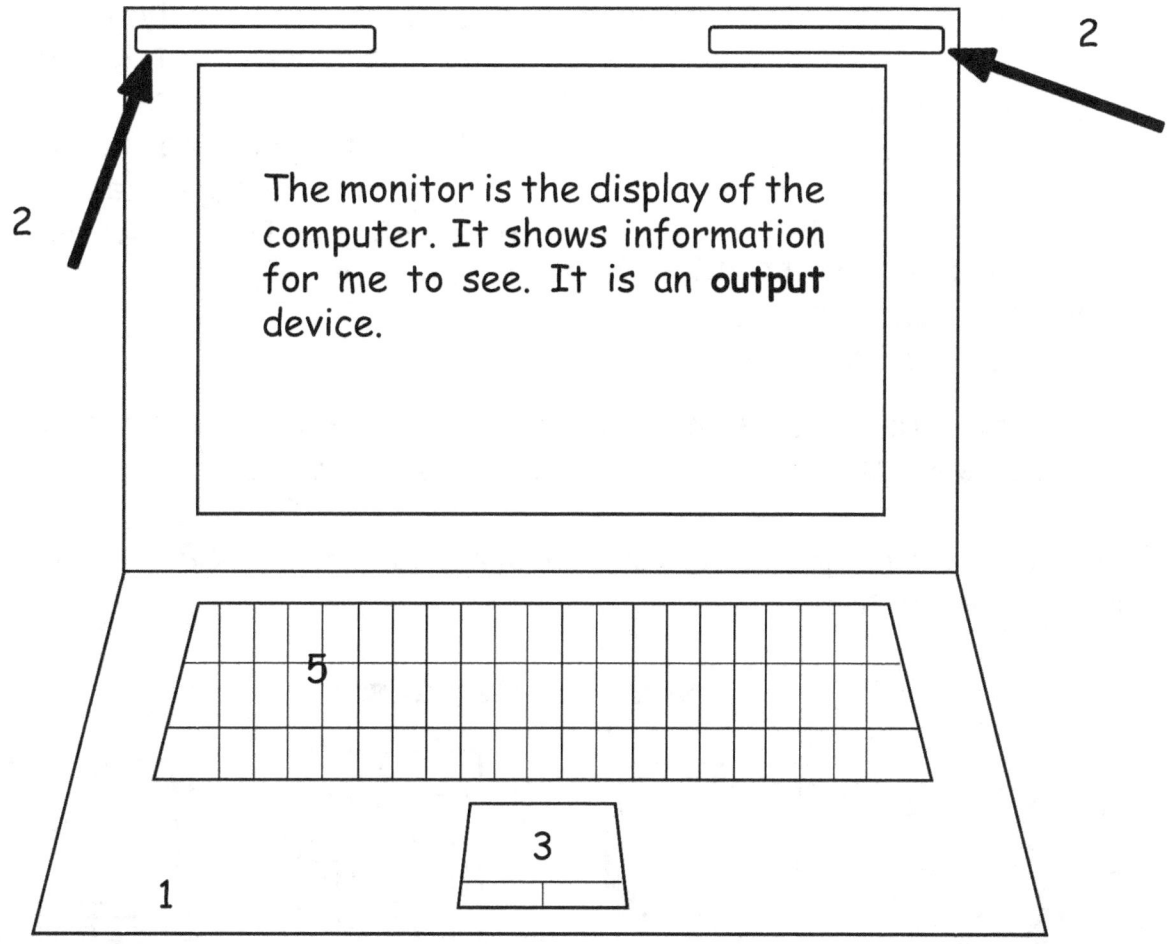

The monitor is the display of the computer. It shows information for me to see. It is an **output** device.

1 The CPU is the "brain" of the computer. It process information.

2 The speakers play sounds that come from the computer. They are an **output** device.

3 The touchpad allows me to move the cursor and click. It works similarly to a mouse. It is an **input** device.

5 The keyboard allows me to type information into the computer. It is an **input** device.

printer 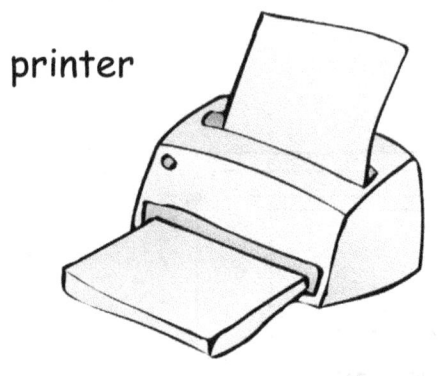 headphones

The headphones play sounds that come from the computer when they are plugged in. You can use headphones in place of speakers. They are an output device.

The printer lets you print information from the computer onto paper.

**Output devices** receive information from the CPU, then translate them into sounds or images that you can understand.

**Input devices** allow me to send information to the CPU to tell the computer what to do.

## Computer Devices

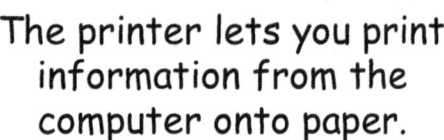

Camera    Computer    iPad    Laptop

Calculator    Stylus    Smartboard    iPod

## Making Connections

Media we hear, read, write, and watch.

| Hear | Read | Watch | Write |
|---|---|---|---|

### Research

When you want to know more about something . . .
1. Ask an expert,
2. Look in a book,
3. Use your computer.

Discuss how each device is used.

# The Internet

The Internet is a network, or system, that connects millions of computers worldwide. It is no longer limited to personal computers. Sometimes simply called "the Net," the Internet can be accessed via tablet computers and most cell phones and televisions. As more and more people use the Internet, the quantity of information continues to grow. Users at any one computer can, if they have permission, get information from any other computer (and sometimes talk directly to users at other computers, like Messenger on Facebook ).

A network, in computing, is a group of two or more devices that can communicate.

Ages 8 and 9 are widely considered as ideal ages to allow kids basic internet access.

## How do kids use the Internet?

Cover the Basics.
Restrict all internet access (without an adult) until kids reach the age of 8 or 9.
Set Internet Usage Rules.
Impact the Right Attitude.
Monitor and Mentor.
Set Behavioral Rules and Limits.
Ensure Responsible Conduct.

Be respectful online. Do not say mean things. Ask before you share a picture or story about someone.

# Online Digital Safety

> **Stay safe online.**

Protect your privacy. Keep Private Information (name, address, phone number, email address, school) to yourself.

Create a strong password. Your password should have a mix of letters, numbers and symbols: ybNm903$.

Do not share your passwords. Never give your password to anyone, except your parents or teacher.

Do not post pictures of yourself.

Do not meet anyone in person that you meet online.

Only visit sites you know are safe.

Tell an adult if you see something that scares or upsets you.

> Cyberbullying is when someone is unkind or hurtful to someone else online. If you are bullied, do not reply. Save every message and tell an adult right away.

# Accessing Information

The library is one type of media center. Media is the variety of ways that people communicate with others. Media is all around us. We get messages from different devices. Learning how to read the messages is important. It is also important that we use it safely too.

The purpose of the media is to inform, entertain, or persuade the reader about a topic.
Persuade - to get people to believe or do something.
Inform - to give people more information or teach them about something.
Entertain - to get someone's attention, usually in an enjoyable way.

## Digital Media

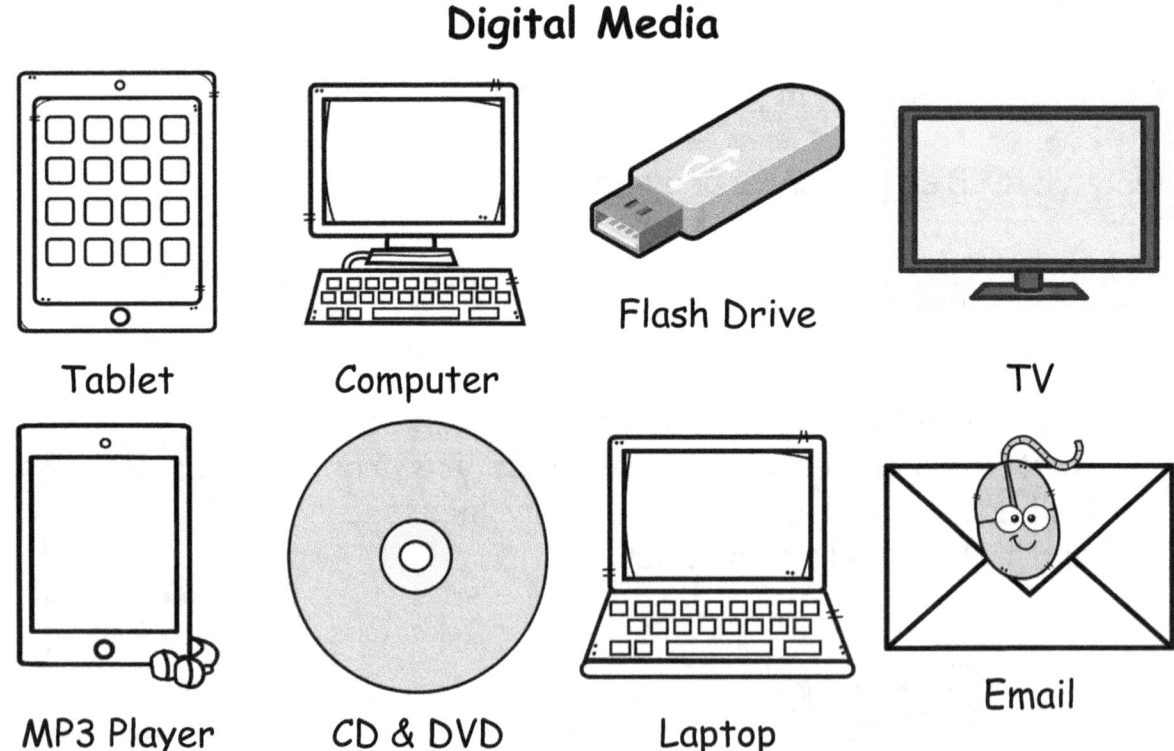

Tablet    Computer    Flash Drive    TV

MP3 Player    CD & DVD    Laptop    Email

## Print Media

Newspapper    Magazine    Book    Signs

## How Writers Influence People

1. Writers use sounds - sound effects, jingles and dialogue.
2. Writers use movements - action, actors.
3. Writers use graphics - images and pictures.
4. Writers use colors - bright and dull.

# How Writers Influence People

### Book

read
refrence
dictionary
pictures
information

### Newspaper

news
pictures
comics

### CD & DVD

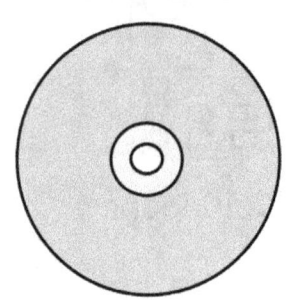

music
movies
audio books

### MP3 Player

music
audio book

### Computer

internet
games
email
websites

### Camera

pictures
videos

### TV

entertainment
commercials
news
weather report

# Technology

Technology are things made by humans to make our lives easier and help solve problems. what would it be like if we didn't have them?

Discuss with students how each item makes life easier and helps solve problems.

# Technology (Then and Now)

How has each technology here made your life fun?

# Comparing Technology

## Technology at Home and School

| Home | School | Home and School |
|---|---|---|
| radio | microscope | camera |
| video game | projector | laptop |
| TV | printer | tablet |
| iron | shredder | calculator |
|  |  | telephone |
|  |  | fan |
|  |  | lamp |
|  |  | toilet |

## Community Workers Using Technology

Together, they can build a house.

carpenter   plumber   painter   electrician

# Technology and Tools

Discuss each tool and how it is used to make our life easier. What will it be like if we didn't have them?

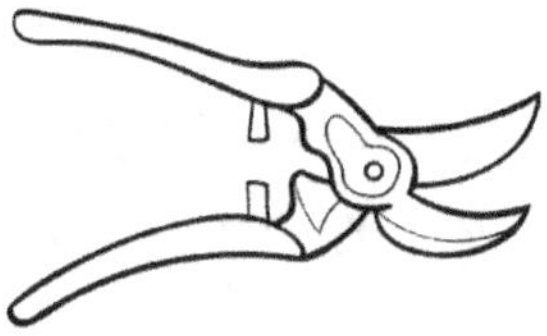

## Technology Spelling List

| | |
|---|---|
| computer | overhead |
| laptop | projector |
| keyboard | calculator |
| mouse | video |
| printer | camera |
| tablet | headphone |
| smartphone | microphone |
| flash drive | ipod |
| marker | earbud |
| internet | iphone |
| shredder | icons |

203

# Primary Bible Lessons

The Bible is very important! It is a holy book that tells how God created the universe and everything in it, and God's love for us. Kinder Kollege Primary Bible Lessons is specifically designed to encourage young students to begin life-long Bible study. All the adventure and spiritual truths of the Bible are skillfully presented in age-appropriate and easy-to-understand language.

Lessons include The Creation, the Golden Rules, Baby Jesus, the Easter Story, the Fruit of the Spirit, Bible Stories, Psalm 23, The 10 Commandments, and 52 Bible verses to memorize.

At the end of the Bible stories, students will get the chance to discuss and show the order of events in each story: First, Next, Then, Last.

# The Bible

The Bible is God's Word. It is a very important book. It tells the truth about God and His world. It is full of stories and they are all true - not fiction.

Even though the Bible is very old, it is still important today. The Bible shows us how to live a good life. It is full of advice, stories, poetry, and so much more. There are stories about evil kings, angels with powers, fire from the sky, and most important, the story about a little baby named, Jesus.

The Bible has 66 books, 39 in the Old Testament and 27 in the New Testament.

## The Old Testament

| | | |
|---|---|---|
| Genesis | Nehemiah | Amos |
| Exodus | Esther | Obadiah |
| Leviticus | Job | Jonah |
| Numbers | Psalms | Micah |
| Deuteronomy | Proverbs | Nahum |
| Joshua | Ecclesiastes | Habakkuk |
| Judges | Song of | Zephaniah |
| Ruth | Solomon | Haggai |
| 1 Samuel | Isaiah | Zechariah |
| 2 Samuel | Jeremiah | Malachi |
| 1 Kings | Lamentations | |
| 2 Kings | Ezekiel | |
| 1 Chronicles | Daniel | |
| 2 Chronicles | Hosea | |
| Ezra | Joel | |

## The New Testament

| | |
|---|---|
| Matthew | 1 Timothy |
| Mark | 2 Timothy |
| Luke | Titus |
| John | Philemon |
| Acts | Hebrews |
| Romans | James |
| 1 Corinthians | 1 Peter |
| 2 Corinthians | 2 Peter |
| Galatians | 1 John |
| Ephesians | 2 John |
| Philippians | 3 John |
| Colossians | Jude |
| 1 Thessalonians | Revelation |
| 2 Thessalonians | |

## The Creation

God is Awesome! God made everything!

**DAY 1**
God made light and darkness.

**DAY 2**
God made water and sky.

**DAY 3**
God made land and plants.

**DAY 4**
God made the sun, moon, and stars.

**DAY 5**
God made birds and sea animals.

**DAY 6**
God made land animals and people.

**DAY 7**
God rested from his work.

# God Made Me

## I am Special

God made me
from my head
to my toes.

He gave me
two eyes and
one little nose.

God made me
extra special,
There is no
one like me!

He made me
part of His
own family!

## God's Family

We are part of God's Family. God's family is led by Him. We are all God's children.

God gave us two families:
1. God gave us a family at home. Our families have mothers and fathers, brothers, sisters, dogs and cats.
2. God gave us a family at church.

## The Golden Rule

How do you want to be treated?

When a friend is hurting,
Don't just watch them cry.
Help them to feel better,
Give it a try!

When it's time to play,
Be gentle and be kind,
Share toys and take turns.
Don't leave a friend behind.

When a friend needs help,
Think of what to do.
Be a friend and help them,
They'd do the same for you!

So. . . how will I treat others?
Do to others what you would
have them do to you.

Get along with others
Help when you can.
Don't tell a lie.
Don't laugh at others.

# All About Jesus

## Baby Jesus

Long ago, God sent the angel Gabriel to a young woman named Mary. He told her, "You will have a son; name Him, Jesus.

Mary was confused; she was not yet married to Joseph. The angel said, "The Holy Spirit will do a miracle, because your baby is the Son of God."

Then the angel told Joseph the same thing in a dream. Joseph's task was to help Mary look after Jesus. Joseph trusted and obeyed God. He also obeyed his country's laws. Because of a new law, he and Mary had to go to their hometown, Bethlehem, to pay their taxes.

It took them a long time to get there because they rode on a donkey. Mary was ready to have her baby. But Joseph could not find a room anywhere. All the hotels were full. Finally, someone felt bad for them and offered them a place to stay, a small barn where animals were kept.

Mary and Joseph were thankful. It was warm, and there was plenty of straw to lay on. That night an exciting thing happened: Mary and Joseph had a baby! But this wasn't just any baby, he was Baby Jesus! The one who would save the world.

Nearby, shepherds guarded their sleeping flocks. God's angel appeared and told them the wonderful news.

"There is born to you this day in the city of David a Savior, who is Christ the Lord. You will find the Baby lying in a manger."

Forty days later, Joseph and Mary brought Jesus to the temple in Jerusalem. There a man named Simeon praised God for the Baby, while old Anna, another servant of the Lord, gave thanks.

Sometime later, a special star led 3 Wise Men from an Eastern country to Jerusalem. "Where is He who is born King of the Jews?" they asked. "We want to worship Him."

The star led the Wise Men to the exact house where Mary and Joseph lived with the young child. Kneeling in worship, the travelers gave Jesus rich gifts of gold and perfume.

Christmas Day celebrates the birth of Jesus Christ.

## Jesus Calms the Storm

One evening, Jesus said to his disciples, "Let's cross to the other side." The disciples got into a boat with Jesus to row across the Sea of Galilee. Soon, it looked like a storm was coming up.

A big storm came up. Waves beat into the boat. It was about to be swamped. The disciples were afraid. But Jesus was asleep in the stern of the boat.

They woke Jesus. "Teacher, don't you care that we are all about to drown?"

Jesus woke up. He said to them, "You are afraid because you do not have faith."

Then, he looked toward the clouds. Jesus said, "Peace! Be still."

The wind stopped. There was calm on the water.

## Jesus Feeds the Crowd

Many people followed Jesus everywhere he went. One day when he came to the beach, he saw a huge crowd waiting for him. Jesus took care of them all day. He prayed with some. He made those who were sick, well. He told them about God's love.

The disciples said to Jesus, "It is late, send them home to eat.

"They don't need to leave," Jesus said. "You give them food."

"All we have is five loaves of bread and two fish," the disciples said.

Jesus took the five loaves of bread and two fish in his hand. He lifted the basket up to heaven and blessed it.

"Here," he said to the disciples. "Feed the people."

Everybody ate until they were full. The disciples filled twelve baskets with leftovers.

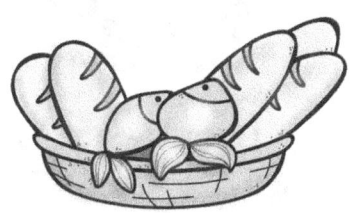

## Who Touched Me?

Everywhere Jesus went with his disciples, a big crowd followed him. One day, in the crowd was a woman who had been bleeding for twelve years. She had spent all her money on doctors. They did not help her. In fact, she grew worse.

She said to herself, "If I touch his clothes, I will be healed."

She touched his clothes. Instantly, her bleeding stopped.

Jesus said to her, "Your faith has made you well."

## Jesus Raises a Dead Girl

"My little daughter is about to die," Jairus said to Jesus. "Please, come and touch her."

But the people said to Jairus, "Don't bother Jesus. Your daughter is dead."

"Don't be sad, Jairus," Jesus said. "Only believe."

Then Jesus went to Jairus' house. The people were crying. Jesus said, "Why are you crying? She is not dead. She is sleeping."

Jesus took the little girl's hand. He said, "little girl, get up!"

The little girl got up and walked around. Jairus was happy again. He hugged his little daughter.
Jesus said, "Give her something to eat."

> Discuss and show the order of events in the story: First, Next, Then, Last.

# The Easter Story

After dinner, Jesus went to the garden to pray. He knew something was going to happen. Some men came and took Jesus away. They dressed him in a purple robe and put a crown of thorns on his head. Then, Jesus carried the cross up the hill. He died on the cross. Darkness came over all of the earth.

When Jesus died, his friends were sad. They put him in a tomb. A large stone was placed in front of the tomb. Soldiers stood nearby to see that no one rolled the stone away.

For 3 days Jesus' body lay in the tomb. Then in the morning of the third day, an angel came and rolled the stone away. When the soldiers saw the angel, they were afraid.

The next morning, Mary and some other women came to the tomb. They saw that the stone had been rolled away. It was empty!

"Where is Jesus?" they asked.

An angel appeared and said, "He is Risen!"

Jesus died so that we can all live again after we die. We have Easter to remind everyone of the day Jesus arose from the dead.

Before Jesus went back to heaven, He told his disciples to tell everyone the good news. Anyone who believes in Jesus as their Savior can live with Him forever in heaven. Jesus died for our sins. But He didn't stay dead. He rose again from the dead on the third day.

And that is the wonderful story of Easter!

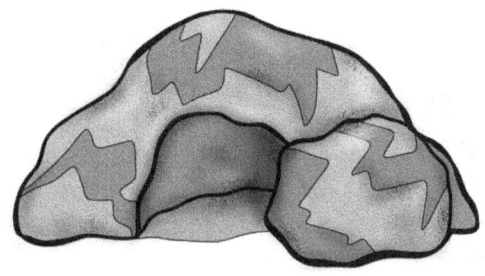

> Discuss and show the order of events in the story: First, Next, Then, Last.

# Psalm 23

The Lord is my shepherd,
I shall not want;
He makes me lie down in green pastures.
He leads me beside still waters;
He restores my soul.
He leads me in paths of righteousness
for His name's sake.

Even though I walk through the valley
of the shadow of death,
I fear no evil;
for You are with me;
Your rod and Your staff,
they comfort me.

Surely goodness and mercy
shall follow me all the days of my life;
And I shall dwell in the house
of the Lord forever.

## The Lord's Prayer

Dear Father in Heaven.
Thank You.
Give us this day our daily bread.
Forgive us our sins as we forgive others. . .
Lead us not into temptation . . .
Deliver us from evil. . .
Thine is the kingdom,
and the power and glory,
forever! Amen.

# How to Pray

PRAISE (thumb) – Praise is telling God how great He is and talking about all the great things that God has done.

THANKS (1st finger) – Thanking God for the things He has done and the things He has given us.

SORRY (middle finger) – Telling God the things we've done that we know He wouldn't want us to do. Tell Him we're sorry and ask Him to forgive us.

ASK (ring finger) – Asking God for the things that we need. This is the time to ask for things we need, not just things we want.

OTHERS (pinky) – We pray for others and it means asking God to help other people. We can pray for our family, our friends, people in our church and other people who need to hear about Jesus.

# Fruit of the Spirit

I let the Holy Spirit produce fruit in my life.  **Galatians 5:22-23**

**Love** - Love means to like very much. We should love each other.
**Joy** - It is good to be happy when someone else wins or receives something. Would you want others to be happy for you?
**Peace** - Getting along with others.
**Patience** - Staying calm when dealing with something that is hard, but needs to get done.
**Kindness** - Show kindness.
**Goodness** - Sometimes we need to think of other people before thinking of ourselves.
**Faithfulness** - Always be a friend when someone is sad.
**Gentleness** - When we use our manners, we are being gentle toward others. We hold doors for people, help them pick something up that they might have dropped, wait our turn in line, and use inside voice when in the building.
**Self-control** - We have control over our actions by standing in line nicely while waiting for everyone to line up.

## God's Laws for us.

1. Love God more than you love anything else.
2. Don't make anything in your life more important than God.
3. Always say God's name with love and respect.
4. Honor the Lord by resting on the sabbath day.
5. Love and respect your mother and father.
6. Never hurt anyone.
7. Always be faithful to your husband or wife.
8. Don't take anything that isn't yours.
9. Always tell the truth.
10. Be happy for what you have. Don't wish for other people's things.

# Bible Stories

## Daniel

Daniel was a good man. He loved God. He always prayed to God. He also obeyed God. He and his friends Shadrach, Meshach, and Abednego refused the king's food when they were just teenagers. They ate only vegetables. The king was not mad because they were honest and hard-working.

As Daniel grew older, he had many important jobs. He was a hard worker. King Darius, the new king, also liked Daniel. This made some men jealous.

The men made King Darius believe things about Daniel that were not true. King Darius ordered them to throw Daniel into a den full of hungry lions. So Daniel spent a whole night in that den.

But God sent an angel to protect Daniel. The angel shut the lions' mouths. Daniel was not harmed by the lions. God was faithful to protect Daniel who had put God first in his life.

## Noah Builds the Ark

Noah and his family loved God. God asked Noah to build an ark and fill it with animals. It rained and rained and rained. It rained for 40 days and 40 nights. Water covered the whole earth.

Only Noah's family and the animals on the ark lived.

God put a rainbow in the sky as a promise that he would never flood the earth again.

## Joseph and His Colorful Coat

Joseph was one of the youngest kids in his family. He had 9 older brothers, 1 older sister, and 1 younger brother. His father loved him very much. One day his dad gave him a beautiful coat. Joseph loved his colorful coat his father made for him.

This coat was made of lots of different colors. Joseph showed his brothers his new coat. Joseph's brothers were angry with Joseph and jealous of his new coat. They were really jealous.

They were mean to him. They threw him into a well, which is a big hole in the ground usually filled with water. Joseph was scared. Instead of hurting Joseph, they decided to send him far away from home. As a large group of people were passing by they sold Joseph to them. He was taken from his family and his home to a land far away.

Joseph finally arrived in his new home. His new home was Egypt. He got a new job. He had to take care of a man named Potipher's house. Potipher was very rich. Joseph was in charge of everything.

One day Potipher's wife wanted Joseph to do something wrong. Joseph said no. Potipher's wife got really mad. She lied to her husband and told him that Joseph tried to hurt her. Potipher became mad and sent Joseph to jail. Joseph spent a long time in jail. God did not forget Joseph.

Pharaoh had a dream and Joseph told Pharaoh what the dreams meant. They had to save food before the famine. Pharaoh made Joseph a ruler in Egypt.

Joseph was able to see his father Jacob again, and save his family from the famine. God had a plan for Joseph to care for his family.

Discuss and show the order of events in the story: First, Next, Then, Last.

# Jonah and the Big Fish

The people living in the city of Nineveh were doing bad things. God had a message for them. God said to Jonah, "Go to Nineveh and let them know that I know what they are doing."

Jonah did not like those people and he did not want to go. Instead, he tried to run away and hide from God. Jonah got on a boat to sail far away. God threw a great wind onto the sea. Soon, a bad storm came and the ship started to sink. Jonah knew this was his fault for running away from God. The ship in which Jonah was travelling was in danger.

Jonah told the sailors to throw him overboard and the storm would stop. Jonah was thrown into the water and started to drown. Even though Jonah was trying to hide from God, God knew exactly where he was. God loved Jonah and sent a big fish to rescue him. The fish opened its mouth and . . . swallowed Jonah!

Jonah spent three days in the belly of the big fish. It was stinky and gross, but Jonah had time to think, pray, and ask God to forgive him.

God forgave Jonah and told the big fish to spit Jonah out on dry land. This time, when God told Jonah to go to Nineveh, he obeyed! Jonah went to Nineveh with the message that God gave him. He told all the people about God's love.

The people listened to Jonah and asked God to forgive them. Because Jonah obeyed, they heard God's message and became followers of God.

> Discuss and show the order of events in the story: First, Next, Then, Last.

# Job

A man named Job lived near Canaan. He was very rich, and also very good. Job and his wife had 7 sons and 3 daughters. Job also owned many animals; sheep, camels, cows, donkeys, and several people worked for him.

Satan felt that Job's life was easy and that was the only reason he was faithful to God. God told Satan he could test Job as long as he didn't kill him.

A servant came to Job and told him that most of his other servants and all of his animals had been killed. Then another servant came to him to tell Job that all of his children had been killed by a great wind. The wind had caused the house they were all in to collapse.

To all of this news, Job tore off his robe. He fell to the ground and said, "The Lord gave and the Lord has taken away; may the name of the Lord be praised."

Satan said that if Job became ill, he would surely be angry with God. So, Satan struck Job with skin sores, causing him great pain.

Job's wife was angry as she lost all of her children and possessions too. Job told her that he will not give up.

Job's friends – Eliphaz, Bildad, and Zophar – came to comfort him. They were concerned that Job must have done something wrong, because itseemed like God was punishing him. However, this was not the case.

The Lord spoke to Job. Because he never turned away from God during his suffering, he was given back his health and belongings. Job was reminded that the Lord could do anything.

# David and Goliath

David lived in Bethlehem. He was the youngest son of Jesse, his father. David's job was to look after the family's sheep. He was a shepherd boy.

The Philistines always fought God's people. Their hero's name was Goliath. Goliath was a big, scary, mean giant. Every day, Goliath made fun of God and challenged God's people to fight him. But, everyone was too afraid to try. David told the king that he would fight Goliath. He knew that God would help him.

David was too small to wear the heavy armor the king offered him. Instead, David chose five smooth stones and took his sling to go and fight Goliath. Goliath laughed at him, but David wasn't scared.

David told Goliath that God would win this battle. David put a stone in his sling, swung it around and around, then let it go. It hit Goliath in the head and killed him. God saved his people once again!

That day, David won a great victory for Israel.

Discuss and show the order of events in the story: First, Next, Then, Last.

# When I'm Afraid

When I'm afraid, like Daniel was in the lionss den, I will trust God to protect me.

I will say my prayers before I go to bed. I will put my trust in God!

**Verse to Memorize**
When I am afraid, I put my trust in You.
Psalm 56:3

When I am alone,
I will put my trust in God!

When lightning flashes,
I will put my trust in God!

When dogs bark loudly,
I will put my trust in God!

When it is dark,
and I feel scared,
I will put my trust in God!

# 52 Bible Verses to Memorize

| | | |
|---|---|---|
| Acts 16:31<br>Believe in the<br>Lord Jesus Christ, and<br>you will be saved. | 1 John 4:19<br>We love because he<br>first loved us. | Proverbs 14:5<br>A honest witness does<br>not lie, a false witness<br>breathes lies. |
| Matthew 22:39<br>You shall love your<br>neighbor as yourself. | Psalm 145:9<br>The LORD<br>is good to all. | Genesis 16:13<br>You are the God<br>who sees. |
| Philippians 4:4 Rejoice<br>in the Lord always.<br>I will say it again:<br>Rejoice! | Numbers 6:24<br>The Lord bless<br>you and keep you. | Colossians 3:2<br>Set your minds on<br>things above, not on<br>earthly things. |
| Ephesians 4:30<br>And do not grieve<br>the Holy Spirit. | Colossians 3:16<br>Let the word<br>of Christ dwell<br>in you richly. | 1 John 5:3<br>This is love for<br>God: to obey his<br>commands. |
| Romans 10:13 Everyone<br>who calls on the name<br>of the Lord<br>will be saved. | Proverbs 3:5<br>Trust in the Lord<br>with all your heart. | Hebrews 13:8<br>Jesus Christ is<br>the same yesterday,<br>today and forever. |
| Psalm 150:6<br>Let everything<br>that has breath praise<br>the Lord. | Romans 3:23<br>All people have<br>sinned and come short<br>of the glory of God. | Matthew 5:14<br>You are the<br>light of the world. |
| Psalm 145:9<br>The Lord is<br>good to all. | Colossians 3:20<br>Children, obey your<br>parents in all things. | James 1:17<br>Every good gift<br>and every perfect gift<br>is from above. |

| Matthew 28:20<br>I am with you always. | 1 John 3:23<br>Love one another. | Psalm 56:3<br>"When I am afraid,<br>I put my trust in You. |
|---|---|---|
| Ephesians 4:32<br>Be kind to<br>one another. | Psalm 119:105<br>Your word is a lamp to my feet and a light for my path. | Psalm 118:24<br>This is the day the Lord has made; Let us rejoice and be glad in it. |
| Psalm 136:1<br>Give thanks to the Lord, for he is good. His love endures forever. | Luke 6:31<br>Do to others as you would have them do to you. | Philippians 4:13<br>"I can do all things through Christ who gives me strength." |
| Psalm 138:1<br>I will praise thee with my whole heart. | John 10:11<br>I am the good shepherd. | Matthew 6:24<br>No one can serve two masters. |
| Proverbs 30:5<br>Every word of God proves true. | Ephesians 6:1 Children, obey your parents in the Lord, for this is right. | John 11:35<br>Jesus wept. |
| Deuteronomy 6:5<br>You shall love the LORD your God with all your heart and with all your soul and with all your might. | Corinthians 10:31<br>Whatever you do, do everything for the glory of God. | Psalm 19:1<br>The heavens declare the glory of God. |
| Genesis 1:1<br>In the beginning, God created the heavens and the earth. | Psalm 139:14<br>I praise you God, for I am fearfully and wonderfully made. | Isaiah 43:5<br>Do not be afraid for I am with you. |

| Ecclesiastes 12:13 Fear God and keep his commandments. | Matthew 28:6 He is not here, he is risen! | Acts 5:29 We must obey God rather than men. |
|---|---|---|
| 1 Thessalonians 5:17 Pray without ceasing. | Isaiah 26:4 Trust in the Lord forever, for the Lord God is an everlasting rock. | Psalm 46:10 Be still, and know that I am God. |
| Proverbs 2:6 The Lord gives wisdom. | Psalm 1:6 The LORD knows the way of the righteous, but the way of the wicked will perish. | Psalm 150:6 Let everything that has breath praise the LORD! |
| Galatians 6:7 Do not be deceived: God is not mocked, for whatever one sows, that will he also reap. | | |

# Kinder Life Skills

# Five Character Traits

**The five character traits to encourage learning.**

Acceptance - talk about acceptance with students; (a) What do they think acceptance means and why is it important? (b) Have them talk about someone who is different than they are. (c) How can differences be a good thing? (d) What is one way they can show acceptance at school? (e) Has anyone ever made them feel accepted? Have them talk about it. (f) What would the world look like if everyone was the same?

Together with the students, pick a few different foods, and try to eat them each with a spoon, knife and fork. Talk about what would happen if we only had forks? Knives? Spoons? Use this activity to talk about how our differences make a stronger community.

Honesty - Here are some discussion points to help you talk about honesty with students. (a) Has anyone ever been dishonest to them before? How did they feel? (b) What do they think honesty means and why is it important? (c) Have them tell you about a time when it was hard to be honest. (d) What makes it hard to be honest? (e) How will others view them if they are honest? How will others view them if they are dishonest? Help students learn the difference between a truth and a lie with this simple game.

You and students take turns saying statements and the other person has to decide if it is a truth or a lie.

Kindness - Here are some discussion points to help you talk about kindness with students: (a) Have them tell you about a time when someone was kind to them. How did it make them feel? (b) What do they think kindness means and why is it important? (c) Who is someone in the class they can be kind to? (d) What are ways they can be kind to people at home, at school and in the community? Spend time writing encouraging notes to each other.

Perseverance - Here are some discussion points to help you talk about perseverance with students: (a) What do they think perseverance means and why is it important? (b) Have them tell you about a time when it was hard to get through a challenge. How did they feel after? (c) What are some things that are hard for them to push through, and how can you help? (d) What are 3 goals they have? What may be some challenges to meeting these goals? What will happen if they don't give up? Help students learn to persevere by engaging in difficult tasks with each student. Find something to do together and commit to pushing each other through the challenge.

Responsibility - Here are some discussion points to help you talk about responsibility with students: (a) What do they think responsibility means and why is it important? (b) Have them tell you about a time when it was hard to be responsible. (c) What is a way they would like to have more responsibility at home? (d) What are their responsibilities in the classroom and in the community?

Help students practice responsibility by giving each student a special job! Let each student pick a special chore each week that they can be responsible for.

# Being Independent

Working independently means you can do it by yourself. It is important for you to do things independently. This means you complete them by yourself. The teacher is here if you need him/her, but you should also try to figure it out by yourself first. It will make you feel good about yourself when you can complete it on your own.

Responsible for Items — take care of your school supplies, don't be wasteful with your supplies and other things. Situations of being wasteful could be taking more food at lunch than you will eat, throwing away paper that could still be used, or throwing away a glue stick that is not empty yet. Some examples of not being wasteful could be saving half a sandwich for later or using the back of a paper to draw a picture. Clean up after yourself and help others. Be more responsible for your items by keeping track of them and knowing where you put them.

Being a Leader and not a follower — it is better to be a leader and lead people to do the right thing, than to be a follower following someone who is doing the wrong thing; doing the right thing for NO reward, and thinking of others before yourself.

# Introducing Oneself

Review how the student is to introduce themselves to someone new. Have them repeat the phrase, "Hello, my name is _____."

# Friendship

Friendship is a warm and kind feeling or attatude toward someone. You can be a friend.

## I am a good friend when I . . .

Give and share.  Help.  Show love.

Care.  Tell the truth.  Listen.

# Telling the Truth

Why is it important that we tell the truth? Are there some instances when lying is okay? Are we still being honest when we only tell part of the truth? Is it okay to leave something out when telling a story?

## What does it mean to tell the truth?

Telling the truth is when you say what actually happened.

If you don't tell the truth it's called telling a lie.

A lie is when you know the truth, but tell a different story. Lying will get you in more trouble than telling the truth. You might not want to tell the truth, because you are scared and you could get in trouble. Telling the truth is always the right thing to do.

Make the right choice.
Just tell the truth!
Always tell the truth.

**Play a game called "True and False."**
Have students make a "true" and a "false" sign, and explain what the words mean.

Now tell students some things that might be true or untrue while they hold up the correct sign for what you say.

Take turns where they say things and you hold up the signs, as well.

# Honesty

Honesty means telling the truth. Telling the truth can be hard, especially when you've done something wrong. But when you tell the truth, you show people you respect and care about them. When you tell a lie, it makes your mistakes even bigger. The opposite of honesty is dishonesty. Dishonesty makes people feel bad. It makes you feel bad too. When you are honest, you can make your mistakes better. You can fix things and get back to having fun. You can be brave and tell the truth. You can say, "I made a mistake, but I'm going to be honest about it." Being honest is hard, but it is an important part of being a good student, family member, and friend. Honesty helps your friends and family, but it helps you, too. You feel better when you tell the truth.

When we are sharing our ideas and experiences, it is best to be honest and truthful about what we are saying. But sometimes when it is time to share our experiences, instead of being honest and truthful, we make up a story that is not true. It is because we want to impress our friends, or make us seem more interesting. Other times, we might be dishonest or make up a story if we want to keep from getting in trouble. We might be dishonest or make up a story if we want to get someone else in trouble. We might be dishonest or make up a story if we are trying to keep a friend out of trouble. We might be dishonest or make up a story if we are using our imagination about what we wished would have happened. We might be dishonest or making up a story if we are embarrassed about something we have done. Being dishonest or making up a story instead of telling the truth when we are sharing ideas and experiences is not a good choice to make. Being dishonest causes the people around us to lose some trust in us. They start to worry that we will not be truthful in other situations too. Sometimes when we make up one story, then we have to keep making up more stories to cover up the first untrue story we told. Being dishonest can also cause someone else to get in trouble even when that person may not have done anything wrong.

Our stories explain who we are. Everyone is different and everyone has different stories to tell. When we make up stories, those stories don't belong to just us, they belong to others too. Your classmates and your teacher will be proud of you if you are honest and tell true stories. You will be proud of yourself too.

Have students memorize The Promise and recite it every day.

### The Promise
Being myself and telling the truth is a better choice to make. It is important to love myself, and to be proud of myself. I don't need to make up stories or be dishonest about what I have done.

## Taking Others' Things

"Finders" does not mean "Keepers". You shouldn't take things that don't belong to you.

## Building Trust

What does it mean to trust someone? Trust means that someone will always be there for you and help you when they can. You know they will be there. How do you build trust? You look at someone when you talk to them, and do what you said you were going to do.

# Positive vs. Negative Behavior

Behavior means the way in which a person acts. We all act in a particular way by what we choose to do. It is good to think carefully before you decide what to do. That way, you select the Good Choice and not the Bad Choice.

## Good Choice = Positive Behavior

Listening to the teacher.
Focusing on your work.
Staying on task.
Staying in your seat.
Raising your hand.

Working together. Giving a high-five.
Cleaning up. Helping a friend.
Being a good friend.

Not giving up.
If at first you don't succeed,
try. . . try. . . try again.

Being appreciative.
Listening and thinking.
Staying quiet in line.
Being responsible.
Using self-control.

## Bad Choice = Negative Behavior

Not working as a team.
Not telling the truth.
Not listening.
Pushing & throwing things.
Using unkind words.

Drawing/scribbling on someone's paper.
Copying someone else's work.
Making a mess. Ripping paper.
Distracting others.

Invading personal space.
Kicking objects or kicking someone.
Teasing. Pushing someone.
Stealing from someone.

# Behavior Sort

Good Behavior     Bad Behavior

Have the students sort out the behavior.

Being neat.

Pushing & throwing things.

Being kind.

Kicking things.

Working as hard as you can.

Caring.

Telling a lie.

Stealing someone's candy.

# Rude, Mean, & "Bullies"
## Be a Buddy, NOT a Bully.

Are you a good friend? Do you use kind and caring words when talking with others?

 Put a list of words on the board. Have students draw and write one word in each ballon, then color the balloons with the kind and caring words.

# Away with Bullying!

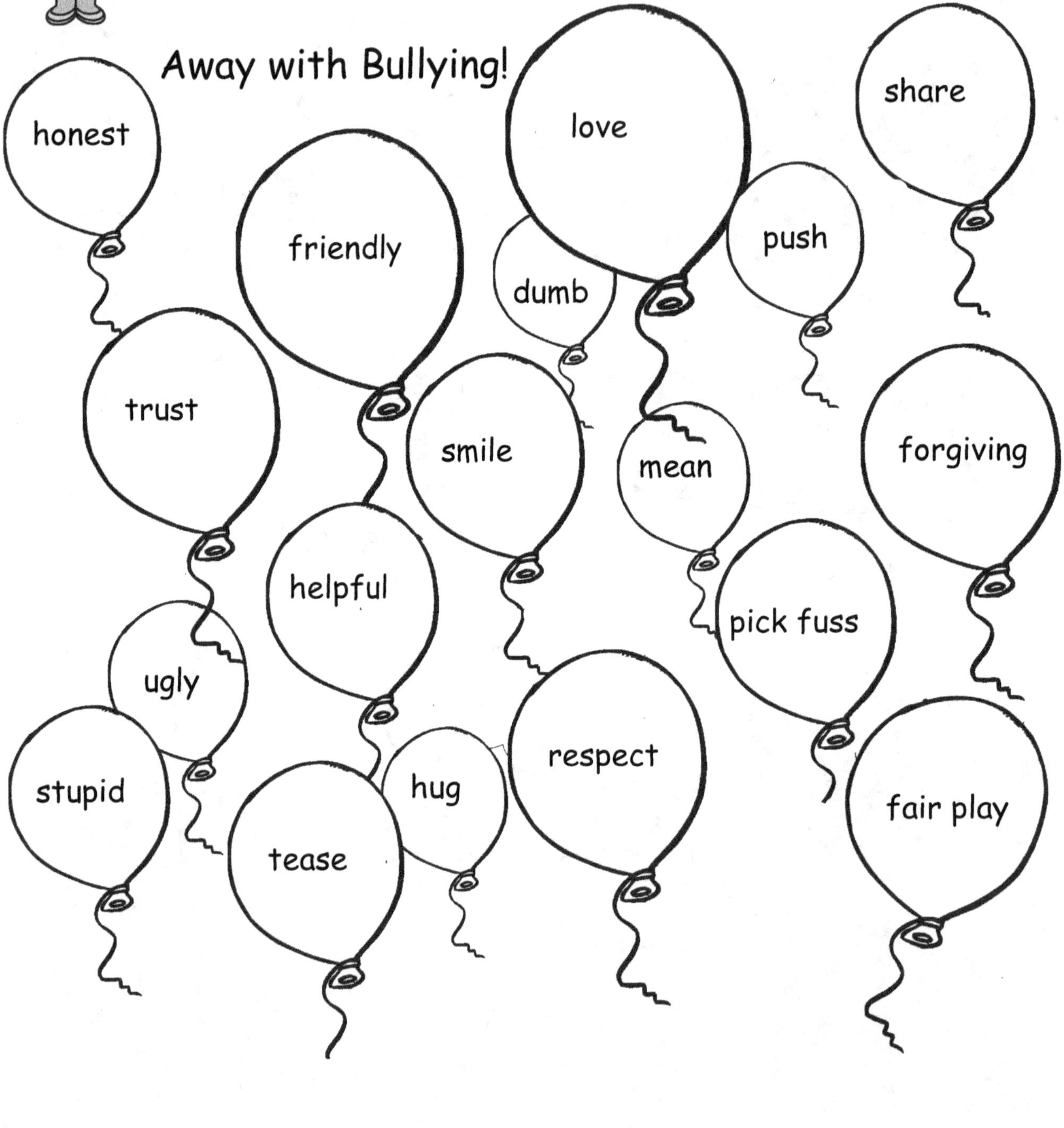

- honest
- friendly
- love
- share
- dumb
- push
- trust
- smile
- mean
- forgiving
- helpful
- pick fuss
- ugly
- respect
- stupid
- hug
- fair play
- tease

# Sad, Mad, or Glad.

When something happens, it's ok for us to be sad, or mad, or glad. It's ok for us to be scared too. Our emotion is like a light bulb.

 When we feel happy and confident, our light shines BRIGHT!

When we feel sad, angry, or upset, our light might be DIM (less bright).

 When your light feels dim, there are things you can do to brighten it! Some of these ideas might help you COPE and some of them might bring you COMFORT.

Cry.
Draw a picture.
Hug someone.
Talk to someone that you trust.
Hug a pillow.
Write about how you feel.
Do something that you really enjoy.
Count your breaths.

 Discuss with students, What to do when something happens.

# Safety

## Crossing a Street
Be careful when crossing the street. First, you must stop. Then, look to make sure no cars are coming. First, you look left, then right, then left again.

## Stranger Safety
What students should do if a stranger tries to ask them questions, lure them towards a car, or asks the students to follow them. Don't answer any of their questions, or say "No" and walk away to tell your teacher or parent.

# Protecting from Illness

## Bathroom Etiquette
The proper etiquette for the bathroom is to be quiet, do your business, flush the toilet, and wash your hands. make sure the paper towels are placed in the trash can.

    (Students should pratice how to wash their hands.)

# Don't Spread Germs

1. Cover your sneezes. If you don't sneeze into a tissue or your arm, you are spreading your germs everywhere.
2. Wash your hands. Turn on the water, get one pump of soap, and scrub. Then, rinse off all the soap bubbles, dry your hands with paper towels, turn off the water and throw the paper towel in the trash can.
3. Use hand sanitizer. Use one pump of hand sanitizer, that is plenty of sanitizer to clean your hands and not make a mess or waste it.

# Protecting from Sexual Abuse

# Hugs & Kisses
We don't ever give kisses at school. It is okay to give hugs at school, but you should always ask first. Make sure it is okay to hug someone instead of just hugging them.

## There are three types of touch.

### Safe Touch
Safe touches are wanted and fun. They make us feel excited, loved, proud, and happy.

Examples of safe touches are hug, high five, pat on the back, holding hands.

### Ouch Touch
Ouch touches hurt us and are unwanted. They make us feel hurt, scare, sad, and angry.

Examples of ouch touches are hitting, punching, throwing things, pinching, kicking, and pushing.

### Private Touch
Our private parts are covered by our underwear. Private touches are unwanted.

They happen when someone touches your private part or ask you to touch theirs. Private parts are called "private" because they are no one's business but our own.

They make us feel embarrassed, confused, disgusted and uncomfortable.

If someone tries to give me an Ouch Touch or Private Touch, I am strong and brave. I look the person in the eye, I tell them, "No, Stop, I don't like that!" in a strong voice. Then I find a grown-up I trust and tell them what happened right away.

### I Can Stay Safe!

I am the boss of my body.
I decide who can touch me, where, and when.

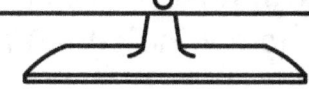

Sometimes Mama, Papa, or a caregiver touch my private parts to keep me clean. That's okay by me.

Sometimes a doctor touches my private parts to keep me healthy. That's okay by me.

It is against the law for a grown-up to give me an Ouch Touch or a Private Touch.

I never keep secrets about Ouch Touches or Private Touches. Even if the person tells me I'll be in big trouble or they will hurt me or my family if I tell. I still have to tell a safe person I trust who can help me stay safe.

# No Secrets!

Always tell a safe person, a grown-up you trust, about ouch touches and private touches.

A small group of people who have permission to care for your personal needs, make you feel safe and respected, and listen to your feelings.

Teacher | Principal

Mama    Papa    Police    Grandma & Grandpa

Ouch Touches and Private Touches are never your fault. When you tell a safe person about someone hurting you or someone close to you, you are a hero!

Think of 5 people you can talk to whenever you don't feel safe. These 5 people will be part of your Safe Circle. Who is in your Safe Circle?

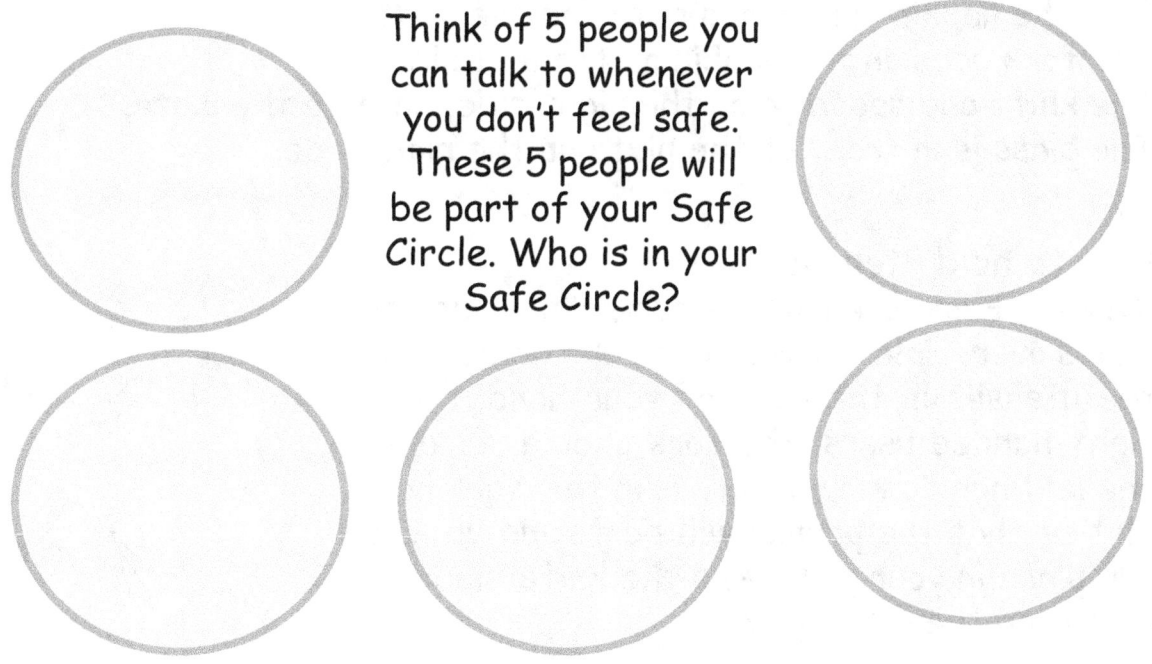

# Table Manners

Good table manners allow everyone to relax and enjoy their meal. Using good manners make mealtime a happy time for everyone. Good manners show respect for others.

Place Setting — this is the way we set the table at dinner time:
1. Take the plate and set it down.
2. Fold the napkin in half and put it on the left.
3. The fork goes on the napkin on the left side.
4. The knife and spoon go on the right side, next to the plate.
5. The glass is in front of the plate on the right side.

## How to hold utensils

(Step 1) Place utensils in your palm. Turn your hands over. Hold out your hand and gently place the utensils in the palm of your hand. For all right-handed users, the fork should remain in the left hand and the knife is in the right hand. Notice that the prongs will be facing up when you place in your palm. And the knife blade will be facing the other palm.

(Step 2) Place and keep the index finger (point the index finger) on the back of the fork and knife and then turn your palm and utensils over. The knife is in your right hand. The index finger is straight and rests near the base of the top. The sharp side is down. The other four fingers then wrap around the handle. The fork is in the left hand. The prongs face downward. The index finger is straight and rests on the back side near the head of the fork. The other four fingers wrap around the handle.

How to use utensils:
(step 1) cut the food using a criss-cross motion; back and forth, back and forth.
(step 2) switch hands. Place the fork in the right hand and the knife on the corner of the plate while you eat.
(step 3) time to eat.
(step 4) time to let your fork and knife rest while you talk.
(step 5) the meal is finished, set fork and knife down to let everyone know you are done.

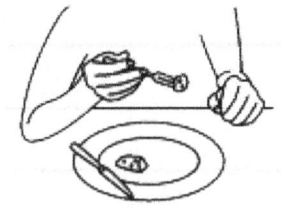

Using your napkin:
First, place the napkin in your lap. When you need to wipe, grab the napkin, wipe your mouth or hands, and then place it back to your lap. Remember, never use your sleeve because that's yucky.

Take out a folded napkin to show the students. Show the students how to gently unfold the napkin, being careful to not rip it. Model how to place the napkin in your lap. Pretend to eat. Periodically take the napkin from your lap, wipe your mouth or hands, and then place it back

243

in your lap. Tell the students that they, too, will get to practice using a napkin. Give each student a napkin. Have them unfold it and place it in their laps. You will role play eating so that students practice wiping their mouths and hands.

Choosing the correct eating utensils: Give each student a fork, knife, and spoon. These can be toy utensils or plastic utensils. Tell students to pick up the utensil they think should be used to eat different types of foods. Give students examples, such as: eating ice cream, putting butter on bread, or eating fufu or boiled cassava. Another option would be to show pictures of food and have students show the correct utensil that should be used.

## When to eat with your hand

Pass out plastic pieces of food or pictures of food. Ask students to hold up the food if they are able to eat it with their hands. Have them put it back down. Then ask if they have a food they would need utensils to eat. They will hold it up if they do. Have them trade food with another student and ask the questions again.

Using good manners at the table: Make sure your hands are clean before eating. Sit still in your chair during mealtime. Take small bites of your food and keep your mouth closed while chewing. Smacking or slurping your food or drink is rude. Chew your food before you talk. Use a napkin when you have food on your face. Ask to be excused if you want to leave the table.

Things you SHOULD NOT do while sitting at the table: Don't speak with your mouth full. Don't use your fingers to eat. No tipping or spilling food. Don't make a mess. Don't throw food. Don't kick under the table.

# Motivating With Passion

## What Makes a Teacher Great!

**Proficient communication skills.**
If a teacher's communication skills are good — verbal, nonverbal, and visual, which involve speaking, writing, imagery, body language, and the organization of ideas into understandable structures — they can convey knowledge with better skill and results.

**Superior listening skills.** Good teachers also happen to be excellent listeners. "If speaking is silver, then listening is gold."

**Knowledge and passion for teaching.**
A teacher is only as good as what they know. Passion is infectious. The love of education inspires students to learn. The best teachers are those that clearly show the love and importance of education, and pass that passion and desire to learn on to their students.

**Ability to build caring relationships with students.**
A good teacher notices when even one student among many does not understand and makes an effort to communicate individually when necessary. A great teacher doesn't only teach from the head. In the best classrooms, hearts are involved, as well. Great teachers need to be able to build caring relationships with their students. It is the caring student-teacher relationship that facilitates the exchange of information.

**Friendliness and approachability.**
Because it's the teacher's job to help students learn, they must be easy to approach. Students will have questions that can't be answered if the teacher isn't friendly and easy to talk to. The crabby, unapproachable, terse, mean, arrogant, rude, all-business teacher don't make good impressions that last a lifetime. If the students think of their teacher as their enemy, they certainly won't learn. The best teachers are the most open, welcoming, and easy to approach.

**Outstanding preparation and organization skills.**
Great teachers spend endless hours outside of the classroom preparing, designing lessons, learning more (both about their subject matter specifically and how to teach, in general), participating in professional development, and thinking of fresh and interesting ways to teach the students. Have excellent lesson plans, lectures, and assignments that they continually improve.

**Good work ethic.**
A great teacher will do almost anything to help their students. They always make time and are always willing to help. If something doesn't work, they'll work tirelessly until they find a solution. A teacher's work is never done, but the best ones never stop trying; they never quit.

**Community-building skills.**
The best teachers understand the importance of building supportive and collaborative environments. Great teachers foster healthy and mutually respectful relationships between the students. They know how to establish guidelines and assign roles to enlist every student's help and participation. Every student feels like they are not only accepted by the larger group, but that their presence is a necessary ingredient in the classroom's magic. Their classrooms are like little communities where each individual plays a part and feels at home.

**High expectations for everyone.**
A teacher's expectations have a huge impact on student achievement. The best teachers have high expectations for all of their students. They expect a lot from each student, but those expectations are both challenging and realistic. Great teachers strive to help each student attain their personal best.

# How to be a Great Teacher

A teacher should serve as a role model for their students. Guide them and when the time is right, let them go as they need to face the world on their own. Being a teacher is like being a parent; you mold students from the start and push them a little bit further when they start to grow. Once they are old enough, give your best wishes and say goodbye. One day, when you two will meet again, you will be surprised by the flashbacks and memories you have undergone with each student and how you have affected his or her life.

1. Be a companion — Be a friend, but always know where you stand and where your limits are. You are a role-model; know when to switch. By this, we mean a teacher should know when is the proper time to be strict. Be their friend, but don't go too far. Help students with schoolwork, listen to them, talk about their lives, but remember you are their teacher.

2. Don't limit yourself to the chalkboard, make your lesson relevant to their lives — If the teacher is not only limited to the blackboard and actually tries to apply what or she is teaching to the students through an activity students can relate to, students might come to understand a certain topic better than before. If you want your students to remember your lessons, try to connect the information you provide with some moments of your students' lives.

3. Use as many different materials for your lessons as possible — Use books, videos, music, presentations, speeches, and everything that can be interesting for your students. Be patient, and explain your material over and over again, making sure all students understand what you're talking about. It would be difficult for them to learn further if they don't get the basics.

4. Be prepared to teach — Organizing time and preparing materials in advance are important in effective teaching. Know your content. Do the reading, take notes on the material, review lecture notes, prepare an outline to cover, make a list of questions to use, make a handout to discuss, design homework assignment or questions, compile bibliographies

or other outside information related to the material, collect visual materials, prepare supplemental reading.

5. Manage the classroom effectively — Managing your classroom includes all the strategies a teacher uses to organize and arrange students, learning materials, space, and use of classroom time to maximize the efficiency of teaching and learning. Establishment fair, reasonable, enforceable, and consistently applied rules. To encourage a positive and orderly learning environment, establish a routine and system for daily tasks and requirements. Use classroom routines as a means of enforcing high standards for classroom behavior.

6. Believe in them — Students who do not believe in themselves tend to have more behavioral and academic problems. A good teacher instills confidence. Teachers who believe in their students and constantly push them to their limits, and appreciate what they are doing are the best ones. It is very important for a student to feel the support of his teacher and know, that he will always help when it is needed. Try to believe in everyone, and don't leave any of your students behind.

7. Don't stop learning — As a teacher, never close your doors to knowledge. Study more about your subject even if you are already a master of it. Don't limit yourself; adding additional knowledge to your lectures can amaze students and make them think that you are so smart, and slowly they can be influenced by you. Show them that you can still work and study at the same time.

# Empowering Students

The act of empowering students is a process of guiding them to feel and believe that they are prevailing as youngsters. When we empower our young children with skills development, they are claiming their right to a decent living by being willing to take the role of leadership. Part of empowering our students is making sure they have the right to give their views and opinions about decisions that affect them and to be listened to. This develops a strong sense of self-esteem as they grow up. Teachers can play a major role in helping students find their voice; having the courage to speak up, express their opinions, (having opinions in the first place), help them discover what makes each of them unique, and help them to define their life goals.

## How teachers can empower their students.

Practice positive reinforcement, and make it a positive experience. Positive reinforcement is anything that occurs after a behavior that increases the likelihood that the behavior will reoccur. You do not want to reward students for just doing what is expected. Be specific in your praise, especially when teaching something at the beginning. Consider what you want students to do and notice who is doing that well. Specify what it is that you like. Vary the recipients of your praise. Positive reinforcement improves behavior. Examples of positive reinforcement: giving high five, offering praise, giving a hug or pat on the back, giving a thumbs-up, clapping & cheering, and telling another adult how proud you are of the student's behavior while the student is listening.

- Invite each student to lead: students should be asked to lead, whether they accept the offer or not. Don't force participation, inspire it. Spark participation with an engaging subject. Keep asking, throughout the year, and eventually, having watched others do it, the student will realize it's not really intimidating. Help students find their passion; passionate people don't remain quiet for long.

- Allow creative expression: students should be given the freedom to voice what they think. Offer more engaging prompts by getting students to speak out on topics covered in class. Give more discussion time for students to explore and develop their ideas—discussion enhances learning and memory. Support innovation, making something new will encourage them to continue thinking about new things. Encourage students to write down new ideas, at the moment, as they arise.

- Recognize those students who speak out: pull students aside and let them know you appreciate their courage or refer to his/her comment later in a class discussion. It's the personal touch that is most rewarding. Encourage students to explain their views; if students can explain why they agree or disagree, they are one step closer to turning all those opinions into a single voice.

- Make lessons personally relevant: it is easier for students to see where their voice might fit into a situation if that situation is relevant to their daily lives. Share inspiring stories, yours or someone else's. The more successful self-expression students see, the more likely they are to try it themselves.

- Allow students to disagree with you: make sure they feel comfortable enough to express their opinion. Encourage casual debate, a debate is one of the best excuses to exercise your voice. Reward risk-takers, a student will find their voice much more quickly if they aren't afraid of taking risks. Welcome feedback on your teaching, one of the best ways to show your student's voice matter.

- Be a better listener: no matter how good we are, we can always be better. Your student's voice depends on it. Inquire— think —reflect is a great voice-strengthening exercise. Have students ask questions on a topic, consider possible answers, and evaluate the accuracy of each answer.

- From time to time, let each student solve a unique problem without making it a competition. This allows students to feel personally connected and responsible for their own issues.

- Promote research as a class project: or an independent project. An opinion backed by research makes for a stronger voice. Brainstorm with your students. Be a part of the process in order to treat all voices equally. It is important to show your students that you do not have all the answers. Having a voice doesn't mean you are always right.

- Recognize performance and progress. Make sure students know the difference between the two and help them understand what you expect. Students can be successful on tasks in class but learn virtually nothing; conversely, students can do relatively poorly on those same tasks but learn quite a lot. Performance is short-term, and progress is long-term. Teachers won't know if their students have actually learned something until after a period of time in which the students didn't use or think about the information. Teachers can evaluate how effective their instructions are by setting the goals, teach, then measure the student's progress toward meeting the goals each week.

- Have patience and let each student finish their thoughts. Don't immediately step in when they are struggling with words. Help students determine what they want. Knowing what you want can lead to knowing what you think. Feeling motivated will help to express it. Build respect for the student's opinion. The student's voice doesn't have to be 'right' or 'popular', but it does have to reflect self-respect. Emphasize that no one gets to know how they feel or what they want if they don't express themself.

- Explore different forms of leadership: leadership can come from art, or teaching others something they know. Teach a lesson on freedom of speech—finding your voice is supported by the law. Emphasize the right to voice their opinion, students should understand that they have a basic right to voice their opinions. Encourage emulation; the best and brightest learn form the best and brightest before them.

- Provide a platform (whether your students like writing, speaking, or building), you'll need to support their means of self-expression with an appropriate platform.

www.ingramcontent.com/pod-product-compliance
Lightning Source LLC
Chambersburg PA
CBHW081741100526
44592CB00015B/2259